POSSESSED
BELIEVERS

Twelve Signs of Possession or Oppression

DAVID HIGGINBOTHAM

ACW Press
Eugene, Oregon 97405

Possessed Believers
Copyright ©2003 David Higginbotham
All rights reserved

Cover Design by Alpha Advertising
Interior design by Pine Hill Graphics

Packaged by ACW Press
85334 Lorane Hwy
Eugene, Oregon 97405
www.acwpress.com
The views expressed or implied in this work do not necessarily reflect those of ACW Press. Ultimate design, content, and editorial accuracy of this work is the responsibility of the author(s).

Publisher's Cataloging-in-Publication Data
(Provided by Cassidy Cataloguing Services, Inc.)

Higginbotham, David.

    Possessed believers : twelve signs of possession or opression
    / David Higginbotham. -- 1st ed. -- Eugene, Ore. : ACW
    Press, 2003.

        p. ; cm.

    ISBN: 1-932124-12-8

        1. Spirit possession. 2. Experience (Religion) 3. Spiritual
    life. 4. Psychology, Religious. I. Title.

BL482 .H54 2003
202/.16--dc22   0309

Printed in the United States of America.

CONTENTS

The Sacrifice of Being Involved in Deliverance
The Authority We Have
We Have to Fight!
Lindi

False Prophets and Dubious Prophecy
Elation and Frustration
Empty Enthusiasm
Falling under the Power of What?
True Worship and Prophesy that Edifies

The Five Senses
Living Faith
Can Faith and Intelligence Coexist?
Intelligent Faith Requires Strength of Character
"That Was Then, This Is Now"

Oscar's Story
Abraham's Intelligent Faith
Quality Faith
Prayers that Really Work

Filling Your House with the Holy Spirit
Does God Discriminate?
What Shall We Then Do?

INTRODUCTION

The truths that I want to share with you in this book come not just from biblical studies or doctrinal statements. They are from experiences with the Lord Jesus Christ that are deeply imbedded in my heart. Of course all personal experiences must be checked and balanced by the Word of God, for it is our final authority on all we do and believe. Yet it is through experience that God brings His Word to life. Often what appears to be a simple, ordinary passage of Scripture takes on new meaning and power for our lives after we pass through struggles and choose to hold onto His promises no matter what. The times that I failed God by doubting and living by my flesh were times of great confusion, but only after finding victories through faith did that confusion make sense in the light of His Word.

I praise God for having mercy on me during the many years as a pastor's/missionary's son. I knew the Bible like the back of my hand, and yet I had no idea how real, powerful, and wonderful God was. "Great Is Thy Faithfulness" and "How Great Thou Art" were just old-fashioned hymns that sounded nice in four-part harmony. Now I sing them from the depths of my soul, because I know how rotten and worthless my life is without the presence of God. Without my struggles and mistakes, I would not have learned how to live by faith.

What I see among Christians today is the same kind of life that I used to live. Knowing the Bible and trying your best to obey God and do what's right does not always answer the many problems with which Satan attacks us. Many sincere Christians have given up their faith, not because they wanted to reject God, but because they felt that it wasn't working the way the Bible always promises. Some Christians who are going through great trials and suffering don't want to be told just to praise God because He works in mysterious ways or that we must just accept whatever comes as His perfect will in our lives. Some Christians are trying their best to praise God no matter what; meanwhile, their soul is in anguish, not knowing how to even begin overcoming their problems.

I know there have been many books written about faith, prayer, and spiritual warfare, and I pray that this does not become just one more book with a "new formula." Instead I want to reveal the truth about how we are to live as children of God in this wretched and deceitful world. I have seen the power of God transform the most miserable lives—from the ghettos of Brooklyn to the slums of South Africa—just by faith alone. God did not call a few to be over-comers, He has not chosen only the "super holy" to see His miracles performed in their lives. He has chosen all of us who humble our-selves before Him and accept Him as our Savior to be mighty war-riors for His Kingdom, tearing down the strongholds of Satan and shining as a city on a hill for His glory and honor. We need only to open our eyes. The prayer of the apostle Paul for the church in Ephesus is the same prayer that I pray for you as you read this book:

> "...that the God of our Lord Jesus Christ, the Father of glory, may give to you a spirit of wisdom and revelation in the knowledge of Him. I pray that the eyes of your heart may be enlightened, so that you will know what is the hope of His calling, what are the riches of the glory of His inheri-tance in the saints, and what is the surpassing greatness of His power toward us who believe. These are in accordance with the working of the strength of His might which He brought about in Christ, when He raised Him from the dead and seated Him at His right hand in the heavenly places, far above all rule and authority and power and dominion, and every name that is named, not only in this age but also in the one to come" (Ephesians 1:17-21).

CHAPTER ONE

My Testimony

I first met Evelyn Sansom at an InterVarsity Christian Fellowship meeting at Rutgers University, where we were both studying in 1982. I was immediately interested in getting to know her since we came from similar backgrounds—although we had grown up in different countries half a world away. Evelyn was born into a Methodist missionary family in Korea where her parents had worked since 1957; my parents had moved to the small African country of Malawi in 1961 as missionaries with the Church of Christ. As I got to know Evelyn through our frequent Bible studies, prayer meetings, and InterVarsity get-togethers, we found that we had more in common than just our backgrounds. Evelyn was sure that God was calling her to do missionary work overseas, which had always been the desire of my heart also—even though preaching was something with which I was not so comfortable. I had been accepted at Palmer College of Chiropractic, and I felt that God would use me through my work as a doctor in the mission field. Evelyn had studied Russian and had done summer missionary work in Soviet bloc countries, and she had a job offer in Yugoslavia to work as a translator for a church there as soon as she graduated. Though it seemed as if we were heading in different geographical directions, we felt the Lord was leading us to each other as we shared the same longing to save souls.

We married in 1983, and Evelyn decided to give up her opportunity to go to Yugoslavia and instead followed me to Davenport, Iowa, where I started chiropractic studies right away. She felt that working together to help me get my degree was the best way for us to begin serving God as we prepared to eventually become missionaries together. Right away, she looked for a job to support us while I was in school. After four years I would be able to start my practice and earn enough money to start a family, at which point we could look into missionary work. We had everything figured out, and it looked like a nice and simple plan to us. We actually felt quite proud of ourselves that we had our lives all in order, and we were sure that God was very pleased with our missionary vision and establishing ourselves financially first.

But only a few weeks after we had moved to Iowa, Evelyn noticed that she was having problems with her vision and discomfort with her contact lenses. When I took her to a doctor, he confirmed that she had a rare eye disease called kerita conus that caused a weakening and disfiguring of the corneas in both eyes. We were shocked and worried, but the doctor assured us that it would take perhaps twenty to thirty years for the disease to gradually develop before she would become legally blind and require cornea transplants. Meanwhile, she needed to be fitted with specialized hard contact lenses, as glasses would no longer be able to correct her vision.

The years that followed were very difficult and painful for Evelyn as her eyes rapidly deteriorated. Many times her contact lenses scratched the surface of her eyes, forcing her to stop work for weeks at a time until new lenses could be made. I remember often coming home to a dark apartment with Evelyn unable to even turn on one light because her eyes felt as if someone had stuck a knife in them. After each episode, the scratches would heal, leaving permanent scars that made the wearing of contact lenses very difficult. Yet without contacts, she could only see objects clearly if they were directly in front of her nose.

Because Evelyn couldn't see, she couldn't work, and because she couldn't work, we had barely enough money to survive. We'd count our last coins, searching all of our pockets just to buy some groceries or put gas in the car. We felt terrible to ask our parents to send us money, but it was impossible to hide from them the dire straits we were in. What a blessing it was to open an envelope with a check from them every now and then as a special "gift" for us. We moved to the cheapest apartment in the worst area of town. Even with the low rent—$100 a month—we would have struggled to pay if my grandparents hadn't taken it upon themselves to help us out each month. At times, Evelyn's contacts would fit well and she would be able to return to work, but all too frequently she would be holed up in a dark room, bored and frustrated and in pain.

I remember the moment that the doctor told me that I had this strange disease. A voice in my head told me that I should pray immediately and have faith to be healed, but another more compelling voice told me that it would be a dangerous thing to do: "You know that the Bible teaches us to pray for the sick, right? But have you ever seen a miracle before? Have you ever prayed for someone to be healed and then seen it happen, just because of your prayer? Have you ever known anyone personally who had been healed beyond a doubt because of prayer alone? In fact, have you ever seen visible proof that God exists (other than what everybody says about how beautiful nature is—but even scientists have pretty good theories about that!)? So what if you pray, and pray really hard, and convince yourself that you're going to be healed...what if NOTHING HAPPENS?! What if you put God on the line—really ask in faith like He says you're supposed to do to receive anything you ask—and He lets you down? How are you going to handle clear evidence that His promises in the Bible are just a bunch of meaningless words or that He doesn't exist at all? You'll have to stop believing in God. You'll never be able to sincerely pray again, and what little faith you already have will go right down the drain. If you pray for healing and nothing happens you'll lose your salvation. Better be careful and pray the 'safe' prayer of healing...you know, the one that goes 'Oh, Lord, let me be healed if it be thy will, and if not let me learn the special lessons of patience and longsuffering through this terrible trial.'"

And so, after carefully and logically examining the options, I chose to pray the "safe" prayer of healing. That way if anyone asked me if I was using my faith to overcome my problem, I could tell them that, indeed, I was praying. But if I was never healed, I could confidently say that it was the will of God.

But one thing I couldn't understand was why God seemed to just abandon us. Why did He allow us to be so miserable? There was no food on our table, and we were buying clothes from the Salvation Army—not to be trendy but in desperate need of things to wear. Worst of all, why did He allow me to suffer so much excruciating physical pain? I didn't feel more spiritual or closer to Him each time my eyes were scratched and I was in agony. In fact, I felt more angry and frustrated with God than any other time in my life.

I was so sorry for Dave, having to deal with this burden. All our shiny bright plans for our future looked pretty dim. He was under constant stress with his studies, and instead of being a help to him I was just one more source of stress in his life. A lot of other married students at Palmer were unable to deal with the demands of the curriculum and ended up in divorce. I knew that Dave was a man of character and had a fear of God that kept him from considering leaving me, but I'm sure there were many times he wondered if he had made a big mistake by marrying me.

After eight tiring months of "church hopping," we settled on a small fellowship of believers who were deeply intent on studying the Bible and, in particular, reformation theology. It was not a church that was involved in evangelism or outreach to the lost or the needy, nor was it a church that dealt seriously with the personal spiritual needs of its few members. It was a church that preached and taught the gospel of salvation through faith in Jesus Christ, and that was good enough for us.

And though I appreciated all the discussions on theology and I learned a tremendous amount about the Bible, it seemed so empty when I could do nothing to help my wife who was becoming increasingly blind as months went by. I told our pastor about how I felt, and he did an extensive study on healing. He was adamant that whatever the Bible says—after examining all the relevant passages in their proper context—we must believe unswervingly in its teaching. His conclusion after many weeks of study and discussion was that the Word of God clearly teaches that we must pray for healing and, if we use our faith, expect miracles from God. For a church that had never prayed for healing and had never seen miracles performed, this was a radical statement, but the Word of God could not be disputed. So, now that we had formed a correct doctrinal and theological understanding of healing, what were we supposed to do next?

Dave's mom and dad were no longer missionaries in Malawi, but they had a church in New York City in one of the worst areas of Manhattan—the Bowery district. They ached to see so many lost and miserable people around them, but the church never grew to more than fifty people. They had a longing for God to do something great in their ministry, to really save souls, to change lives, and to make a difference for Jesus in New York. Their traditional Church of Christ teachings that they had grown up with were ineffective in bringing God to life for their church members, and they were eagerly seeking some new direction from God on how to win souls and grow their church.

They used to call us every weekend from their home in New Jersey, telling us about the seminars on evangelism and spiritual revival that they were attending. Every new book or class excited them and gave them hope to see big changes. But for all the formulas they tried, they saw practically no change at all. Dave's mom was always a fighter and was determined to find God's answer. She told me numerous times that she was convinced God had much more for us, but somehow we were all blind and couldn't see what He was trying to show us. She became interested in ministries of miracles, healings, signs, and wonders and bought all the books and tapes she could find. Dave's dad began to send us all they were reading and learning, and we became equally as fascinated. It was as if, finally, someone could show us how to go about using our faith to find my healing.

But these teachings were so foreign to me. Name-it-and-claim-it teachings were the most common, but I felt like they were reducing the Bible to a formula or a trick to manipulate God into healing. The pastors spoke in such grandiose fashions, as if they knew God better than anyone else. I was skeptical to say the least. But their testimonies seemed real, and they were the only ones I knew who actually saw true healings in their ministries. I couldn't just write them off because I didn't like the way they spoke, but when I tried to pray and act as they instructed, it seemed so insincere.

One pastor who really caught our attention, and who was able to explain miracles and healing in a far more acceptable way, was John Wimber, founder of the Vineyard Christian Fellowship churches (which are now part of an international denomination). Through his more methodical and less "hyped-up" studies, we were able to understand how our minds, spirits, and physical bodies are all intertwined, and how each aspect affects the other. He explained demonization, healing, and using our faith to see miracles through prayer. But it seemed that his ability to pray for all these things came through words of knowledge and prophecies that he received regularly from the Holy Spirit. This is where we were stumped, because we had never heard any voices or divine messages before. I prayed to receive them, but nothing ever came. I didn't know if everybody was supposed to hear voices, but I knew that most Christians did not. If that was the only way to know God's direction, I would never know how to pray, and probably never get healed. One idea was to search for a "prophet" who had the gift and see what he had to say. But who could tell whether his words were really from God or not? Why would God expect us to pray for healing and make it so complicated? I really had no idea what God wanted me to do.

In August of 1986, my dad called me to say that they had found an amazing ministry from South America that performed all kinds of healings and miracles and that cast out demons! The founder of this church, which had about three hundred congregations in Brazil at that time, had come to New York City to meet with other pastors and to see about opening a church in the U.S. The man's name was Bishop Edir Macedo. During that meeting, Dad said that he felt the Holy Spirit moving so powerfully in his heart that he stood up and told Bishop Macedo that he would personally invite him to work in New York—and that he would turn over his church to make the bishop the head pastor, thus making Dad the assistant pastor. I was completely bowled over! When Mom got on the phone, she was still in shock. However, she felt sure that it was not just Dad's emotions getting carried away but that it was truly the Holy Spirit leading them to finally find the answer to their prayers.

In September Bishop Macedo invited my parents to visit his main church in Brazil and find out firsthand what the Universal Church of the Kingdom of God was all about. He was giving them a chance to back out of their offer; he knew that if they weren't wholeheartedly convinced that his ministry was from God, it would be better for him to find another sponsor. They returned from Brazil on fire! Dad felt as if God had given him a new life and a new vision. They came to see us in October with an excitement I had never seen before in my parents. They were in their fifties but were acting and talking like they were twenty years younger.

Their stories of all the miracles they saw with their own eyes were incredible. They told us about demons they saw manifesting in the church and how the pastors and church assistants there all knew how to drive out evil spirits by faith in the name of Jesus. They spoke about a kind of courage they saw in the people of that church in Brazil—a courage that had no fear of facing Satan head-on, by their faith, and destroying his power in their lives. They told us testimonies of healings, of former drug dealers and gangsters who were now pastors with happy families, of witchdoctors who had been delivered from legions of demons and who are now faithful and loving Christians, of paralytics walking, of blind people seeing, and many more stories of the power of God that blew my mind.

If it had been anyone other than my dad telling these stories, I would have been very skeptical. But Dad was a pastor who was always careful with his beliefs, and he was firmly rooted in the Word of God. He would never accept heresy or anything that went against the basic teachings of salvation by faith. While he was in Brazil, he methodically weighed all he observed of the teachings and practices of the church against the Scriptures, and rather than finding a wayward cult, he found a new revival of faith within himself. The Word of God had become more real and alive than ever for my parents— and they had been faithful missionaries for thirty years. The beautiful stories of the past were no longer just stories that needed a stretch of imagination to believe. They were reality.

From the moment we heard what Dave's mom and dad had to say about their new experiences with God, we were sure that was the church for us. Dave had only a few months to go before his graduation, but we couldn't wait to move back to the New York area and see it all with our own eyes. I had been longing to hear all these things for my entire life. I had always wanted to believe in God wholeheartedly, but, from the time I had been saved, an element of doubt hung over me that perhaps the Bible really wasn't the truth.

I had given my life to Jesus when I was thirteen, and I really experienced a change in my heart and in my desires. I had felt strong emotions inside of me that made me sure Jesus was right there in the room with me, holding me in His arms. I began devouring the Bible and praying constantly. That was when I knew that I wanted to be a missionary some day.

But when I turned fourteen, my family returned to the U.S. for a year-long furlough. All the peace and joy I had in my heart dissolved into terror as I entered my first year of high school in a public school in Indiana. I prayed and read my Bible more fervently than ever, but the feeling of God's presence wouldn't come back. I never was able to adjust to the peer pressure, the gossip, and the backstabbing that went on daily in my school. I came home and cried every single night of that year, begging my mother not to make me go back the next day. My mom felt terrible for me and would pray with me every night before going to bed, but nothing changed.

The more I prayed for God to help me, the more desperate I became. It was as if the wonderful feeling of God's love for me was only reserved for first-time converts; the rest of my life I would have to endure whatever misery came my way, because, like the Bible said, the road was supposed to be hard and narrow. It was becoming obvious that God really didn't want to answer my prayers for help: I was praying incessantly, but the kids in school were just as mean, my clothes were just as ugly, and the peace I was longing for never came!

Then another thought entered my mind: Maybe God really didn't exist. After all, there's no real proof that the Bible is true. My parents were good Christians and dedicated missionaries but had never seen a real miracle in their entire lives. They said that they had seen answers to prayers, but nothing so amazing that no one could doubt that it was God alone who had done it. I looked in the Bible and saw Jesus healing lepers, raising the dead, calming storms by a word, turning water to wine, and casting out demons. It was absolutely nothing like the lives of the Christians who lived all around me. Pastors never preached that we should cast out demons (even though Jesus commanded those who followed Him to do so), heal the sick, command a storm to stop, or raise the dead. Pastors would always find some "more spiritual" lesson for us to take home, such as, "the storms of worry and doubt that rage in our minds must be calmed by our faith in the Lord."

But how could I have faith in the Lord if the only evidence I can find is a two-thousand-year-old book and a temporary emotion that is wonderful but only lasts a year? What I ached for in my life was **power**—*power to overcome enemies and power to prove that God was the only true God, like Elijah did with the prophets of Baal on Mt. Carmel. I wanted to walk without fear, do everything with confidence that God was going to help me, speak with boldness, and live completely free from all the pressures and chains of this evil world. I wanted to see real, honest-to-goodness miracles. I wanted proof that God was exactly who the Bible said He was.*

For the rest of my years in high school and college—both in Korea and as an InterVarsity executive committee member in Rutgers—I could never shake this thought from my mind. I couldn't bring myself to deny Christ and turn my back on being a Christian just because I had no empirical proof, but at the same time, I could never bring myself to truly believe in any prayer that was made, no matter how badly I wanted to.

Sitting at my kitchen table in Davenport, Iowa, and seeing a fire in the eyes of my mother- and father-in-law, I felt a new faith kindled inside of me. They recounted how a demon-possessed woman picked up a church pew holding five men and spoke of the evil that the demons were doing in her family; the demon cowered in fear and was cast out when the name of Jesus was spoken with faith. The woman was healed and immediately returned to her normal state of mind and healed. This was the power of God at work. This was the power I had been seeking all my life. This was proof that God was real and active, and I wanted Him alive in my life more than ever!

December of 1986 finally came and I graduated as a doctor of chiropractic. Mom and Dad came for the graduation ceremonies and helped us drive our stuff back to New Jersey. As soon as we arrived, we visited the church with great expectations for Evelyn's healing. Dad's congregation was a bit skeptical and unsure of this radical change in church leadership, but they were happy to see us return home. We also met Bishop Macedo and his family, and we were eager to see all kinds of miraculous signs following him around. Instead, we saw a simple and happy family, patiently trying to learn English and get used to life in the U.S. But when Bishop Macedo began to speak with the use of a translator, we were amazed. He would say things like, "Either God exists, or He doesn't. Stop trying to be an in-between Christian, claiming to believe in God, but never taking the risk to see His power at work in your life." That was exactly who we were—in-between Christians.

Bishop Macedo loved challenges. He loved challenging himself, and he loved challenging others to put their faith into practice. One thing that struck me about everything he taught was that he was so sure the Word of God was true that he had no fear of putting it on the line. I always knew that Dad—and other pastors I had looked up to—had believed that the Bible was true, but not the way Bishop Macedo did! He had no qualms about telling people that it was God's will for them to succeed or be healed or blessed in all they did, as long as they put Him first in their lives. He spoke about Gideon, Joshua, Moses, and Abraham as if God expected us to do the same miracles today that they did in their time. He taught us that we should stop waiting for God, that God was waiting for us to make the same radical decisions of faith that those men of the past did— to sacrifice all, to lose our life for the sake of Christ in order to gain great victories for God's glory.

Bishop believed wholeheartedly that the way Jesus spread the gospel through miracles, healing, and powerful teachings was exactly the way the church today must spread His Word. Witnessing through the Bible and trying to convince people to be saved is not always enough to rescue those who are suffering from the hands of the devil. Revealing God's power in our own lives through miracles is the best way to show the world that God is real and His Word is true. If we desire blessings or success or healing, it should be to glorify His name, to shine for Him for the great purpose of saving other souls. But if we want to see His miracle power, we have to be willing to give our lives and desires to Him and be fools for this world. If we are too proud and want to pick and choose how we would like to follow Him, He will never stop loving us or trying to help us, but we will never see Him manifest the greatness of His power in our lives, as He desires.

This was when many of Dad's old church members began drifting away. They still loved Mom and Dad, but this new teaching was too much for them. I can't speak for each one, but it was clear that many didn't want their lives to be challenged—to give their all for Him for the sake of saving the lost. They weren't interested in seeing miracles if it meant that they had to confess their own weaknesses and humble themselves before God.

Eastside Church of Christ had been such a cozy, friendly place, with monthly potlucks, weekly Bible studies, and lots of hearty hymn singing. It was a well-integrated church with whites, Korean immigrants, families from the West Indies, African-Americans, Chinese, and Hispanics. Uptown yuppies mixed with the occasional homeless person off the streets that Dad was earnestly trying to save. For many evangelical Christians, this was a picture of a solid and well-rounded church. But for Mom and Dad, a congregation of fifty in a city of millions, where so many were living in suffering, this church was far from what God wanted them to do.

It was confusing and saddening at that time to see people whom we had always regarded as strong, mature Christians recoiling at the idea of making the church grow and explode by revealing the power of God through miracles and healing. Bishop Macedo taught us that if we want to do great things to save others, we have to look into our own lives first. We had to be honest and consider the possibility that even we who believe in Jesus may be unaware of evil spirits working in our lives. It was a radical statement for me, but as Mom, Dad, Evelyn, and I examined ourselves, we decided that if the devil was working in us in some way or another, we wanted him to get out! We weren't going to pretend that we were super-Christians no matter how many years we had spent serving God. We wanted to start anew.

The second week we were in the church, Dave stayed in the basement one night conversing with Bishop Macedo and his father. When we got in the car to go home, he quietly told me that Bishop had called him to leave his career and become a pastor. I smiled and thought, "Now isn't that sweet?" But when I looked at Dave, I saw that he was seriously thinking of saying yes. He told me that Bishop asked him if he wanted to be a doctor or a pastor.

"I said, 'both,'" Dave explained, "since we always wanted to be missionaries, but he said that there was no time to be both—either one or the other. He said that if I chose to remain a doctor that God would bless me, but if I chose to become a pastor, I would be blessed much more."

Dave smiled, waiting for me to jump up and say, "Go ahead, Dave. Let's do it!" Unfortunately that was the last thing I wanted to say. I was really frustrated because all my life I had promised God that I would do whatever He asked of me—that I would sacrifice whatever it took, even my own life, to obey Him. I always saw myself as a person who had no love for the material things of this life, and I was pretty proud of myself for it, too! If God had called us at any other time in our lives, I would have been so excited and thrilled to jump at the chance. But, after four years of living in poverty as a struggling student couple, I was looking forward to all the comforts of being a doctor's wife that I felt I deserved, and I didn't want to hear anyone talk about sacrifice right then.

I was also a bit ashamed to come back to the East Coast after working so hard to get Dave through school. So many people were calling and congratulating him on his graduation and asking when he would begin working as a doctor. I hated the idea that we would look like fools and fanatics, throwing twenty-five thousand dollars worth of student loans down the drain just as he was ready to launch a great career.

It seemed like the most ridiculous and illogical request to call Dave into the ministry at that time and place. But deep in my heart I knew that it was not just the call of one man to another, but it was the voice of God Himself. If we said no to this, we would be saying no to God. And when I looked into my husband's face I could see that no matter how many logical arguments there were against going, he had already said yes to God in his heart—and there was no turning back.

And so I began my hands-on education of how to work as a pastor. I was baptized in the Holy Spirit a few weeks afterward. The church was small and it was difficult to get an understanding of what I was supposed to do, so, as he had done with my parents, Bishop sent Evelyn and I to Brazil for ten days to see the church there and get a better understanding of the ministry. We came back transformed. We saw demons manifesting for the first time in our lives. We talked to many pastors and their families who had been healed and delivered from the worst problems; even after many years of being saved and blessed, they were still walking testimonies of the reality of God's power. They were so confident and bold—so unlike ourselves and most of our American Christian friends, who were always cautious in talking about God to unbelievers so as not to offend anyone.

We were amazed at the miracles of healing that we saw in Brazil and hoped that God would choose to heal Evelyn while we were there, but we came back to New York without the one miracle we wanted the most. By that time Evelyn's eyes were at their worst. The doctors could not fit her with contacts anymore because they were too painful for her to wear. She had become legally blind. We weren't too discouraged because we knew that we were in the right place, learning about faith, and we believed that soon enough she would see again. If all these other pastors and their families had been healed of deadly tumors and all sorts of problems, Evelyn's eyes would be healed easily—or so we thought.

Months went by, and we found out that Evelyn was pregnant with our first son, Todd. We were both concerned about how she would care for him once he was born, but we kept telling ourselves that God would heal her soon and everything would turn out okay. She was trying her best not to complain about the disease, and when people asked her how she was doing she'd always smile and say that she was fine. But sometimes at home she would cry and get discouraged. We prayed a lot, but I couldn't figure out why nothing was happening. All I could tell her was that God would do it at the right time.

Meanwhile I was getting frustrated with her condition. I had responsibilities to carry out at the church, and I needed to be ready and available for any work I was called to do. But Evelyn was unable to go anywhere on her own. Even walking down the stairs was frightening for her because, unable to see where she was walking, she had fallen a few times. Crossing the street to buy a few groceries at the corner store was a harrowing experience, especially since we were living in one of the most dangerous neighborhoods of Brooklyn. Washing and ironing were practically impossible, although she tried, and housecleaning was a hit and miss attempt at getting rid of dirt. The worst was seeing her just trying to exist day by day. She normally liked getting to know people and conversing with newcomers in the church, but because she couldn't see them she hardly interacted at all with the members. I felt pretty alone at times, as though I had to take care of home and the ministry by myself.

Evelyn's Healing

One thing that I knew I couldn't do was to stop praying for miracles to happen in other people's lives. The power of God that I had seen in Brazil was becoming a reality in my own life through my ministry in the church. God was teaching me day by day how to use the authority that I had over Satan and his demons, to cast them out, to heal the sick, to bring people face to face with the truth of God's existence and bring them to repentance and salvation. It was a time in my life when I felt that I finally really knew God. For all the years that I had read the Bible and professed a faith in God, it was not until 1987 that I experienced true conversion. The fact that Evelyn wasn't yet healed couldn't stop my excitement nor the conviction that God had led us to the best life we could ever have: serving Him as a pastor with real answers to real problems. I didn't know why she wasn't healed, but I knew that I never wanted to go back to my old life.

Being in Universal Church was a thrill for me, too. Seeing people walk in the door of the church sick and in pain then walking out completely healed made me want to burst with excitement. I wanted everyone to know how great God was and that He could heal and change anyone's life. As years went by and Todd got older, I was determined to teach him all the wonderful things that I had never learned as a child. Every time demons manifested in the church, I would explain to him how the devil is at work in the world, and when they were cast out, I wanted him to see that the Lord Jesus was so much greater and stronger than any evil thing we see. I was praying in a new way, using my authority to overcome problems as I never had before. I was confident of God's desire to bless everyone who had faith, and all those doubts and questions of whether or not He existed had been firmly and permanently wiped out of my mind. After living a life of fear and anxiety, the inward changes that I went through were like breaking out of my shackles. And yet I still wasn't healed.

Todd's birth had been as wonderful a miracle as any mother and father go through to see their little one come into the world. He was perfect and healthy in every way, but, unable to see him correctly, I constantly worried over him. I would hold up his face to my eyes to see him as best I could and carefully inspect him all over with my nose to his skin, making sure nothing was hurting him or wrong in any way. Every time he made the slightest sound, I would rush over to him, imagining how terrible it would be if he were really in pain and I didn't know how to help him because of my blindness. I tried my best to be a good mother and pastor's wife, and to keep up my faith that God would heal me some day. I tried to always tell people that I was fine, that I had nothing wrong with me, so that God would see me using my faith and heal me quickly.

But sometimes it got to be too much: Caring for a baby was exhausting; cleaning the house and doing laundry seemed to be a losing battle; and going to church with a big smile on my face, telling people that God was going to bless them and answer their prayers was more of an act than sincere encouragement. My attempts at having a strong faith were more like a roller coaster ride than anything like real faith at all. I would listen to sermons on the power of God, how we have to believe and act on our faith, and I would leave the church full of gusto and determination to see my healing happen. Many times I would go home and tell Dave, "Now things are really going to change. Now I'm **really** going to use my faith, and **this time** it's going to work." He'd look at me with an appropriately serious face, nod his head vigorously, and say, "Amen, I believe." But I knew that he was only saying that because he had to. After about four or five days of claiming my healing, walking around with a very determined attitude, and taking great care not to say anything that sounded as if I had any doubts, I would start to lose steam. It was too hard to keep up the act of the "soldier of faith," and the reality that I was still as blind as a bat was too much to ignore. Keeping myself in a constant state of forced happiness and repeating "I believe, I believe, I believe…" in my head all the time became unbearable!

But when I saw that I had slipped in my attempt to have faith, I would proceed directly to an emotional crash. I would cry bitterly for days, knowing that I was a miserable failure when it came to having faith. I was supposed to have a faith that persevered, but I could only last a few days. I was supposed to be sure of what I hoped for, but I was so confused. I was supposed to be a pastor's wife, able to teach and counsel and be an example in the church. Instead I was a disgrace. I knew that if I wasn't healed it was my fault and not God's fault, but I

was trying so hard. I had been faithful and doing my best to serve Him
in our ministry through the years, I knew the Bible well, I had never
committed a terrible sin as many of our church members had in their
past, but still God was refusing to heal me.

Those times of depression lasted for months. I felt that there was no
one to whom I could explain my feelings. When I tried I would break
down and cry so much that I preferred just to keep quiet. Even Dave got
tired of hearing me agonize over my situation, so I'd keep up my act in
front of everyone and try not to think about my blindness too much. I
decided it was better not to pray too hard for healing and instead be
patient to wait for God to heal me in His own time.

In the spring of 1989, Bishop Macedo and a group of other bishops
and pastors from churches in South America came through New York on
their way to Israel for a special meeting. One afternoon as we were all
gathered together, Bishop called me over as he was talking to the men.
He asked me if I remembered the story of Jesus spitting upon the ground,
making mud, and smearing it on a blind man's eyes. After the man
washed off his eyes he was healed. Bishop felt in his heart that we should
make that same sort of prayer for my healing right then and there,
together with all the other pastors, if I was willing and also had faith. I
said I did, although my faith was dragging pretty low that day. They all
spit on their hands, lay them on my eyes, and made a fervent prayer on
my behalf. I cried as I remembered how long I had been struggling, making the same sorts of prayers, and finding nothing. When they finished,
Bishop said to me, "Evelyn, don't worry any more—you are healed. Go
to the doctor quickly and he'll give you good news. Do you believe?" I
said yes very firmly and thanked them, wiping the tears from my face,
but when I saw that my vision was exactly the same as it had been
before, I thought it would be best just to forget the prayer ever happened.
If I went to the doctor and he told me that my eyes were terrible and only
surgery would help, I would sink into another depression again and
maybe never come out. Even so, I was grateful that they tried.

A few months later, I was with David in our Brooklyn church for a
3 P.M. service. Few people had attended, but it was a powerful service.
A drug dealer with a painful sickness had been brought by his mother
and brother. There was a woman who had lived her life like a prostitute, with various children from different men. Though these people
had lived the worst kind of lives, they had faith enough to seek help from

God. Both of them manifested demons during the prayers, and it was a great opportunity for Dave to show the rest of the church members who the devil really is and how great and powerful our God is. As the demons were cast out of these two people, both of them felt completely different than they had before. The drug addict tried to find the pain he had carried with him for a long time, but it was gone. The woman also was healed of a long-standing problem. I felt that excitement again as I witnessed God at work in the lives of those who cry out to Him. I was so blessed to see people walking out of the church with smiles and a new-found faith in God. I remember standing at the door as I wished them good-bye, praising God in my heart for what He had done.

At that moment, a longing for my own healing came over me, and I spoke to God in a way I never had before. "God, I am a pastor's wife. I am a much better Christian than those people who just left. I have known you and known the Bible since I was a child. But they have walked out of here healed, and I will walk out of here blind. Please, God, tell me: What do they have that I don't have? What did they do that I haven't done?"

And as I searched my heart, God answered me—not in a voice, but in my thoughts. "I healed these people because they believed in Me like a child. They didn't question or analyze or try to figure Me out. They came to Me in humility with open hearts, and that's all I ask for." His answer was so simple and so clear, the work the Holy Spirit was doing in my heart at that moment was staggering. God wanted me to learn from a drug dealer and a prostitute. God had chosen them to be my teachers, my examples, and I wanted more than anything to have the exact same faith that they had. I felt so free and full of joy when I saw how the answer had always been there. My own foolishness had blocked God from healing me. I had treated faith in healing like a formula to be followed to the last drop, but God just wanted me to treat Him as my Father who loved me.

The first thing I told Dave when we got home was that I wanted to make an appointment to see the doctor immediately. Bishop and all the other church leaders had prayed for me and proclaimed my healing. He had given me orders to go to the doctor, but because I thought I knew better I had not obeyed. But now I understood that God had already answered their prayer—it was up to me now to do what I was told and believe.

The following week I saw a specialist, who told me that my eyes were badly deformed and that I needed to sign up on a waiting list for a cornea transplant right away. He told me that it would be a process of at least two years. First I would need to wait for a donor, a recently deceased person with healthy corneas. After surgery on one eye, the transplant would leave me in bandages for a few weeks, with pain and sensitivity to light lasting for a few months until the eye stabilizes. Nine months or a year later—and depending on the availability of another cornea donor—I would be ready for an operation on the other eye, and the process would be the same. There was no guarantee that the operation would improve my vision, though many who have had the transplant can see much better than before. There was also the risk of complications during the surgery that could leave me permanently blind. On top of all this, it would cost me handsomely! He recommended that I see one other colleague of his for a second opinion, and then come right back to begin proceedings for surgery.

I had no intention of going through this operation. We couldn't afford even a fraction of the cost. At any other time, this diagnosis would have sent me out in tears, but, strangely enough, I was elated! I had a joy and an assurance in my heart that something wonderful was about to happen. I felt a peace that made no logical sense whatsoever; it came naturally rather than being forced.

As the days went by, the peace in my heart never wavered no matter what happened around me. The next doctor examined me and told me that my eyes were too far gone for any kind of lens to fit, but thought he would like to test out a hard contact lens just out of curiosity. Fitting a contact lens requires a cornea with a normal curve. My corneas were no longer smoothly curved as healthy ones are; instead they were lumpy like mountain ranges, with swirls of scar tissue from old abrasions. But when he popped in his trial lens, I saw again—with no pain! For the first time in two and a half years, I saw my hands, my clothes, my face in a mirror. The lens fit my eye perfectly. He was amazed and wondered how it could be possible, but he said that surgery was definitely out of the question as long as lenses could help. One week later I returned to pick up my first set of contact lenses, and I left his office seeing well enough to drive a car.

Seeing eighteen-month-old Todd for the first time was amazing, as was seeing Dave's face again, the leaves on the trees, and the clouds.

Even the garbage on the streets of New York was beautiful to me! The most amazing thing of all was that I had begun (only begun) to learn what true faith is and how eagerly our Father in heaven wants us to love Him and trust Him as a child would. Finally, after six years of struggling with this disease and struggling to know God's will for me, I had found healing.

Today I live a normal life. I still wear contact lenses, but with each visit I make to the eye specialist, the condition of my eye improves. This is a disease which is said to never reverse or improve, a disease that only worsens. Yet for some medically unexplainable reason, my eyes and my vision are constantly getting better.

But what I am happiest for—and I am very happy about my eyes—is that I have found a new relationship with Jesus. All those months and years that I was depressed and crying over my blindness, I thought of myself as a victim, that God was ignoring me. Only later could I see that I had been ignoring God. I had always believed in Him as my Lord and Savior, but I had never really known Him. I wasn't listening to Him. When He required my faith, I gave Him my own imitation of faith, like a performance, doing and saying all the things I had read in books. When He required my love, I gave Him anger and frustration for not giving me what I wanted. When He required trust, I stopped praying because I was sure of being disappointed. I didn't know it, but I was just as wretched and worthless as any other sinner who had committed the worst crimes.

But when I understood how much He loved me—and how much He longed for me to be in communion with Him, to break my pride so I would simply trust in Him as a child with her Father—I gained so much more than physical healing. I found the answer to every prayer I have ever made or will ever make.

Since Evelyn's healing, we have gone on to many more challenges and struggles in our lives and ministry. But the lessons that God taught us during her search for His answer are still very much a part of our lives today. God wants health for his children; God wants us all to live abundant lives, overflowing with blessings. But more than anything, He wants us to know Him intimately—to trust in Him and to live in total dependence on Him. Without this, all the riches, health, and blessings in the world would be meaningless.

Neither our knowledge of the Bible, our years of faithful church membership, our attendance at Christian seminars, our presence on the InterVarsity executive committee, nor our upbringing in Christian missionary families had any value in the eyes of God if we did not have true communion with Him. Even the fact that I was a pastor who could cast out demons was not enough for God to answer our prayer. God took us through a desert to drive us close to Him, and even though He knew it was painful for us, the end result was that we found a deep relationship with Him that has only grown deeper with time.

> "...that he would grant you, according to the riches of His glory, to be strengthened with power with His Spirit in the inner man, so that Christ may dwell in your hearts through faith; and that you, being rooted and grounded in love, may be able to comprehend with all the saints what is the breadth and length and height and depth, and to know the love of Christ which surpasses knowledge, that you may be filled up to all the fullness of God" (Ephesians 3:16-19).

Fighting Demons in Africa

After serving God as a pastor for six years in New York and New Jersey, the call came unexpectedly: "Pack your bags, you're leaving for Johannesburg, South Africa, in a week!" Evelyn and I were astounded at the news. Africa had been home to me from two years old until fourteen, and it had always been my dream to return. But Evelyn's parents, after forty-five years in the mission field, had just retired and moved to a small town on the coast of New Jersey—to be close to us. In fact, they had just bought their new house and were waiting for us to come and visit them when we got the call. The thought came to our mind, as it had years ago when we were first called into ministry, "Why now, Lord?" We both loved the idea of being missionaries and traveling to far off lands to serve God, but it was a crucial time for her parents as they adjusted to a completely new life at sixty-seven years old. It seemed cruel to abandon them. Evelyn's brother lived in Minnesota and her sister in Georgia; they were unable to step in. But God was calling us, and if it truly was His voice, we couldn't say no. As difficult as it was to explain to our families, we packed four suitcases and a backpack of toys, and the three of us were on our way right on schedule.

Arriving in Johannesburg in 1992, we found a country perched on the edge of its first democratic elections. The ruling white apartheid government had become obsolete due to political international pressure and sanctions, and the black leaders, led by Nelson Mandela were preparing to take over the helm after their inevitable win in the coming months. The atmosphere was clearly tense among the minority whites who owned most of the businesses and controlled most of the money. They had, directly or indirectly, enjoyed their prosperity at the expense of the poor and abused black manual laborers, who had been treated no better than slaves for the past three centuries of white colonialism.

The country did not look at all like what I remembered of my childhood home of Malawi. Back then, the white neighborhoods had been off limits to blacks and "coloreds" (mixed race), except for maids and gardeners who worked for their white masters. These areas looked as beautiful and luxurious as any high-class neighborhood in Los Angeles or Palm Beach. Downtown Johannesburg had also been a white-only territory; blacks could only enter during daylight hours to work in the businesses and shops located there, and only if they had special stamps in their passes to authorize their presence. The black neighborhoods were called townships or locations, where blacks had been resettled; the men were forced to work in the dangerous gold and coal mines, and the women were taken to become housemaids. These townships were crowded with shacks built of cardboard, corrugated tin, bits of plywood, and scrap metal. A few had electricity and running water, but most had nothing but candles, firewood, and water gathered from the communal water tap. Some who had more money had actual brick houses with tile roofs, but these were still a world away from their white South African brothers living in wealth and comfort.

Just months before our arrival, however the pass system had been abandoned, and the laws of separation eradicated. Whites and blacks were, for the first time, legally free to travel and live wherever they chose within the country. Poor blacks from the townships and rural areas swarmed into Johannesburg, eager to find some sort of work and an opportunity to change their miserable way of life. Whites were, on the whole, terrified. The term "white flight" was commonly heard on the news as white South Africans packed their belongings and moved to Europe or Australia to escape an impending civil war. For the blacks and coloreds, it was a time of great hope for a better life; for whites, it was a time of great anxiety and fear of retaliation.

We drove our rental car out of the airport onto a modern super-highway—replete with billboards, heavy with traffic, and flanked with large office buildings and factories. As I walked through the streets of Johannesburg, I watched many black men and women selling small piles of farm produce on the sidewalks, trying to earn a few *rand* to support their family. I saw all sorts of street vendors, manual laborers, office workers, and beggars crowding the streets. And no matter whose eyes met mine, their faces would immediately break into a beautiful, broad smile—as if we had been long lost friends. Instead of hatred toward whites, I saw kindness and a willingness to become friends. It wasn't what I expected; after all they had a right to be angry and suspicious of all whites. But, contrary to what I had been told, I found a very open-hearted society.

I also saw that South Africa was a land of two different worlds. The contrast of people was amazing. A white couple dressed in imported European clothes climbed into their new Mercedes without a thought for the African woman who was slowly making her way past them. She carried a bundle of homemade clothes on her head and a sleeping baby on her back as she spread out her wares on the sidewalk for sale. Each day as Evelyn and I looked at our African brothers and sisters, we heard the voice of Jesus: "For as long as you have done it to the least of these, my brethren, you have done it unto me."

I knew that God had something great to do among these people who were in such suffering. We searched newspapers and classified ads for a location to begin our church and soon found an empty basement, which had previously been a supermarket, right across the street from the Johannesburg train station. With constant badgering—and a lot of prayer—we convinced the owners to lease it to us. We got the keys on Christmas Day and began to clean and prepare for our first meeting on January 3, 1993.

The advice of other pastors, whom we sought out for guidance, was not encouraging. "Please, don't rush into this." "You're making a big mistake!" "Wait until after the elections." "Get your family out of here—don't you know there will be a civil war?" What struck me was that none of them had any ministries helping the black South Africans, only the whites. When one pastor heard that I planned to open a church primarily to reach out to the blacks, he cautioned me: "They are a strange and dangerous group of people. They have their own mystical religions and witchcraft that only another black person could understand, and they are very violent—they'll kill you!" But the more they tried to discourage me, the more I felt sure that I was doing exactly what God wanted me to do.

As other missionary pastors and their families came to join us from our churches overseas, we went ahead with our plans. We advertised a healing service in a local newspaper, and we were amazed to see two hundred people attend our first service. Right away, people were healed of longstanding sicknesses, and the news spread quickly. We held services three times a day for the next few weeks, and in two months we had crowds of a thousand, pressing themselves into any small corner they could find to listen to the Word of God and receive prayer for their problems. The basement had no windows and the walls were literally dripping with sweat. With seating space for only six hundred, we soon had to add two more services per day to care for all the people who came. After each service, we had long lines of people waiting for special prayer and counseling, but before we could finish, more people had come into the church ready for the next service. We had to move the counseling lines to the side while one of us began preaching again.

Every day was exhausting and exhilarating. But the most incredible thing was that we were seeing lives actually change. Healings from blindness, tumors, paralysis, and other sicknesses were happening daily. We would photograph them and ask permission to use their testimony for the newspaper ads, and when the news of the healings spread, more people flocked to the church.

It had been many decades since white missionaries had been allowed to work freely among the black South Africans, and we were quite a novelty. In the first few services we held, we could feel racial tension and fear. The people were unsure of how I would treat them or what I would expect from them. But as we learned to sing in Zulu, Xhosa, and Sotho, they would enthusiastically join in with dancing and surprised appreciation that we cared about their culture. Day by day we laid hands on all who came, we counseled them, and we treated them with love and respect—and the curious visitors became faithful members.

Our manner of attracting people to the church was to appeal to their need for help. Our catch phrase on all our advertisements and flyers was "Stop Suffering!" It was the perfect attention grabber, because the majority of black South Africans lived—and still live—in abject poverty and were in a great deal of suffering. But in a way, we also were appealing to their traditions of looking for quick fixes to their problems through witchdoctors and herbalists. Many who came to our meetings thought that we were just another spiritist, or *sangoma* as they called them, with special potions to cure their ills. But instead, we prayed for them in the name of Jesus, taught them the Word of God, and showed them that there is no spirit or power greater than the Lord Jesus Christ.

Convincing them that Jesus Christ was the strongest was easy—but convincing them that the spirits of witchcraft and ancestor worship were demonic was not. Though many enthusiastically embraced our church and loved attending our meetings, there were always a good many who would still consult their sangomas on the side, just to cover all their bases. We did not want to become just another healer or witchdoctor in their eyes, but, on the other hand, it was impossible and unreasonable to expect them to come to church with only the holiest of motives. We had no problem with the idea that thousands would come to our services because they were looking for stronger *muthi* (witchdoctors' medicine), but, once we had their attention, we had an obligation to teach them the truth about salvation through Jesus Christ alone.

Speaking out against ancestor worship, idolatry, and witchcraft became a normal part of each service, as we tried to show people that the devil works through these things to enter a person's life to destroy him. Even sangomas began to attend the services because they heard that some of their clients had been healed by the power of Jesus Christ. Though some thought they could learn how to gain our new "powers," they began to understand the message of salvation and to see the destruction of the evil spirits that they thought were their dead ancestors. Soon we had a storage room full of old witchdoctors' clothes, talismans, chicken bones, dried herbs, horse-hair whips, and all the other trappings of the sangoma's trade. Each time the piles got too high, we would have a giant bonfire. And as others gave their lives to Jesus, they also gave up their past and everything with it. Some afternoons our assistant pastors had the strange job of pouring bottles of whiskey and beer down the drain, as our members would clean out their homes and their hearts.

But true conversion is far more than turning away from witch-craft or addictions; it is a life of denying our flesh and walking in loving obedience to our Savior—day by day, step by step, until our last breath. This really is the narrow path, which is sometimes painful and never easy but so full of blessings and joy that even the difficulties become a pleasure compared to the cheap pleasures of this world. This task of bringing true conversion —teaching people who had never known the truths of the Bible and who had been immersed for generations in spiritism and the occult—was one that would take time and perseverance. But if we, as pastors to these suf-fering people yearning for an answer to their problems, did not have the patience to bring them to true conversion, we would all be fail-ures in the eyes of God.

We were not the only church that worked among the black South Africans; every mainline church in the country had ministers and congregations in the black townships. The Anglicans, Lutherans, Methodists, Presbyterians, and the infamous Dutch Reformed Church (that created the "doctrine" of apartheid based on its inter-pretations of Scripture) were all represented in the black locations. While counseling a church member, I asked if he or she was a Christian. People would often respond yes and name the church to which they belonged. But when I asked people why they were so mixed up in the sangomas and ancestor worship, they told me that they had never been taught by their churches that it was wrong.

While reading a magazine put out by the World Council of Churches for Africa, I came across an article stating that ancestor worship is not in conflict with Christianity because it is ultimately a way for an African to reach out to God. As an African prays to his dead grandfather, he will speak to the spirit of his father, who will, in turn, speak to his own father, and on and on until the last one speaks to God about his descendant's problem down on the earth.

Their reasoning was that since the message eventually reaches God, praying to their dead relatives is not idolatry but legitimate prayer. The article went on to explain how our Western culture must not impose itself upon others and that sensitivity to the African tradition is important for spreading the gospel. What kind of gospel they were referring to is beyond me! Suffice it to say that though roughly 95 percent of those I have counseled called themselves Christians, only a small minority of these knew that ancestor worship and consulting witchdoctors was demonic.

Why these churches chose to turn a blind eye to all the spiritism going on in their midst has never been explained to me, but I can speculate that the supernatural healings and powers that the sangomas displayed were beyond the scope of understanding of these very traditional churches. Though they had the Bible and all its teachings, they did not have anything even close to the miraculous power that the Africans experienced in witchcraft. Convincing an African to abandon his traditions would require having something stronger and more powerful to offer. If churches have no more than Bible stories, ethics or politics, a sangoma with promises of healing or prosperity has much more influence. And, in truth, witchcraft does have a lot of power. People have died, suffered terrible diseases, found marriage partners, and seen their enemies' businesses collapse—all due to rituals done by sangomas and the demons that they send. To call witchcraft just a primitive deception of uncultured people is a grave mistake made by many Western Christians; the power of the devil is not something to be ignored.

So, baffled by the strange pagan practices of African tradition, churches preferred to stay within their own liturgical comfort zones and leave the unexplainable to the side. It was because of this situation that we needed to show the miraculous power of God—through healings, deliverance from evil spirits, and testimonies—and allow for people to make up their own mind who the true God is. As we expected, news spread quickly throughout the black townships that there was a church with powerful white "sangomas" from overseas who could perform miracles. Though we were happy to see thousands respond so quickly, packing the services until there was no place to stand, we fully understood that most came out of curiosity and a desire to see something supernatural—just as the crowds must have followed Jesus and His disciples. Bringing them into the church was easy with the powerful miracles that happened. Getting them to deny their flesh, pick up their crosses, and daily follow Christ was a completely different task.

Rumors spread, which still circulate even today, that our pastors are actually "spookies" or zombies—dead bodies inhabited by evil spirits, who perform miracles to deceive the living and possess their bodies. Reports went that we asked people to close their eyes during the prayers because the pastors actually flew around the church (casting evil spells) and that we put snakes under everyone's chairs to bite them (causing them to scream). A pastor in Nelspruit, a town on the eastern border, had to face the gossip that he, a 180-pound fellow, flew around on a teaspoon as his wife prepared human flesh for them to eat to gain the healing powers they had. We all laughed and were perplexed at the ridiculous rumors, but sadly they held a powerful influence on many of the black South Africans we were trying to reach. But through years of teaching, discipleship, and lots of love and care, real men and women of God arose to become assistants, pastors, and even bishops.

Within that first year we were able to transplant a significant amount of missionary pastors and open ten churches in the Johannesburg area, one in Durban, and one in Cape Town. As years passed, we expanded throughout the country, opening churched in predominantly black areas—townships such as Soweto, Alexandra, Kayalitsha, Kwa-Mashu, Thembisa—and in the city centers close to the mini-bus ranks, or taxi-ranks as they call them. We became a well-known name among blacks, but very few whites even knew of our existence. By the time I left Africa in May of 2001, we had more than 200 churches in South Africa and 150 more spread throughout the continent from Nigeria and Ethiopia all the way south.

In 1995, Evelyn and I were sent to open a church in the Philippines, where we began all over again. Finding a church to rent, handing out flyers on the streets of Manila, and placing ads in the local newspapers brought in a slow stream of Filipinos who had been steeped in Catholicism. Their willingness to open up to a new ministry such as ours was far more cautious than that of the Africans, but by the time we returned to Africa, a solid church had been established that has now spread to five other congregations under the leadership of other missionary pastors. In the Philippines, just as in Brazil, New York, and Africa, we saw demons manifesting and being cast out, incurable sicknesses healed, and lives transformed by the power of Jesus Christ.

Yet the greatest thing that I saw, during all those years of ministry overseas, was the power of faith. Though I came to Africa and Asia to teach and reveal Jesus Christ to the lost, it was those very lost who showed me how great and loving God is. As the sinful woman and drug dealer had been Evelyn's teachers as she sought healing, the African people were my teachers as they held on to the Lord Jesus to bring them out of suffering and into blessed and abundant lives. Their trust in our counsel was so wholehearted, their belief that God was real and able to solve their problems so unswerving, that I was blown away by the strength of their faith. Because of the potent combination of humility and determination that characterized the Africans' way of living, explosions of miracles happened beyond what I had ever experienced.

Here in this prosperous United States, humility is seen as a weakness and that level of determination is rarely found. And though we have a wealth of knowledge, resources, entertainment, and comforts, we are a spiritually poor and pitiful nation. Walk into any of our churches in the poorest sections of South Africa and you will find smiling, dancing, singing, rejoicing people who are not afraid of what the devil can do because they have lived under his oppression for years. They have found the incomparable power of the Lord Jesus setting them free and reversing the destruction of their past. It is this power that we all need to see at work in our lives, and it is this undoubting faith that will bring it to pass. The incredible manifestation of God's power that I witnessed in Africa is needed now, more than ever, in our own United States. What God has been doing there, He most certainly wants to do here.

CHAPTER TWO

Do Demons Exist?

Nightmares and insomnia had bothered Ann, a woman in her mid-thirties, for fifteen to twenty years. The nightmares troubled her so much that she avoided sleep, and she frequently stayed awake for three to five days in an attempt to evade them. Late at night she'd wash clothes, clean the house, watch TV, or read a book—anything to occupy her mind and make the hours pass until daylight. Toward the end of these spells of insomnia, she'd be so exhausted and careless that she'd find herself in the middle of terrible fights and arguments, involved with men that were no good for her, or going back to old addictions of alcohol and cigarettes.

In addition to the sleeplessness, she would feel the presence of someone in her house when physically there was no one. She would feel something brush her cheek or feel a rush of wind as something passed by her. At times her deceased grandmother would appear to her in visions and call her name. She explained that she and her family had always attended church and were all believers. But she had serious trouble with immoral thoughts, was constantly getting involved with abusive men, and had no children and no husband even though she was desperate to have both. As I laid my hand on her head to pray there was an immediate reaction. Ann pulled away, looked straight at me, and demanded, "What do you want from her? She's mine! You can't have her."

───────────

The last sixteen years have been amazing for Evelyn and me. Experiences like Ann's and tens of thousands of others have been daily reminders of the existence of Satan and demons—and of the mighty power of the Lord Jesus to set oppressed people free. I cannot stress how much these experiences have changed my life. Knowing the cause of the evil around me—and the authority that I have in the name of Jesus Christ to tie it up and drive it away—has transformed me into an alive, excited Christian.

The fact that evil spirits manifested in Ann and wanted me to leave her alone shouldn't seem strange; we can read about similar experiences in the Gospels when Jesus confronted evil spirits. Sometimes they manifested in their victims and spoke to Him. At times they even demanded to know what He had come to do to them.

But if that was the reality in Jesus' time, what about now, in the twenty-first century? Can we expect to see the very same things today? Is the Bible relevant in modern times or is it an out-dated book that only teaches us moral and ethical standards? I doubt that any Christian would come out and say it that way, but in actuality, many live their lives as though the Bible was full of irrelevant ideas. Demon possession seems to be considered a bizarre and rare occurrence today, and most Christians would probably say that demons have no bearing on their lives other than in bringing temptations. But by saying that, we are indirectly declaring that much of what Jesus and His disciples did was useless.

The Word of God is not, and never will be, outdated. It is "living and active and sharper than any two-edged sword" (Hebrews 4:12) and as such will forever be the supreme source of guidance and wisdom. Whatever the Bible treats as important, we'd better treat as important as well.

I'll never forget the feeling I had when I was first introduced to healing, deliverance, and the true power of the Holy Spirit. I said to Evelyn, "It's just like in the Bible! This is exactly what Jesus did!" For years I thought that finding a church like those in the first century was a hopeless dream, something that had been lost forever. But now I know that God is ready to do everything that He's written in His Word. I know this not only because I've read it, but because I've seen and experienced it.

Evil Spirits Are Eternal

From the Bible it's absolutely clear that evil spirits existed before and during the time of Jesus. Why wouldn't they also exist after His life on earth? It makes no sense to say that they no longer exist. They do, and one proof of it is the state of the world around us; there is no shortage of wars, poverty, disease, and violence. John 10:10 says, referring to the devil: "The thief comes only to steal and kill and destroy." As long as there is stealing and killing and destroying, demons are present.

What many fail to realize is that the same spirits that the Lord Jesus Christ cast out are still roaming the earth. Demons are former angels that joined in a rebellion against God, led by Lucifer. They are fallen angels, yet as angels they are spirits without a body. They are created beings, yet beings that will live forever. They cannot be killed or destroyed. Stakes through the heart, cloves of garlic, crucifixes, sunlight, magical spells, potions, and silver bullets have no effect on them whatsoever. The only effective weapon against them is faith—faith in the Lord Jesus.

So when we ask the question, "Do demons still exist and work in this world?" the answer is a resounding "Yes!" They are an ugly, permanent part of this physical world. Only in heaven will we be free from their influence, yet even then they will be alive, tormented in the lake of burning sulfur.

Their future is doomed. There is no repentance for them because they have already seen God and lived in His presence, and yet rejected Him. More than that, Jesus' sacrifice on the cross was

for mankind not for angels; therefore, they have no hope of anything good in the future. If they could, they would kill themselves to
avoid the fires of hell, but they can't. So they do the next best thing,
which is to bring as many others as possible with them to share in
their suffering. That's why the devil and demons attack any and
everyone. Whether a person is good or bad, evil spirits want them
to suffer just because *they* are going to suffer.

I witnessed a similar example of this attitude in South Africa.
When some men found out that they had been infected with HIV,
they became so angry that they went out and slept with as many different women as they could. Their twisted reasoning was, "If I have
to die from this disease I'm going to take as many women with me
as possible." It may seem incomprehensible to you, but I personally
spoke to many people who had this attitude. The reasoning behind
the suffering that demons cause in this world is exactly the same.

Characteristics of Evil Spirits

Because they are spirits, demons have no size, color, or language. I've prayed for people who had one or two spirits inside of
them, and I've prayed for people who had hundreds, even thousands, of evil spirits living inside them. There is no limit to the
number of demons that can inhabit a single person's body because
they aren't limited by size or space. But the more evil spirits a person has, the worse his life is because each one comes to bring more
suffering and pain.

Demons speak and understand all languages. I've prayed for
people whose language I didn't know, but the spirits inside of them
understood my prayer and had to obey. Though the people did not
understand my language, the spirits inside of them did. At times the
demons would pretend not to understand, yet because we know
that they are liars and are not limited by things like language and
space, as we insisted they responded to our commands. I've even
heard manifesting demons speak English through the mouths of
people who don't know English.

Demons work in every nation of the world. They're not limited
to Africa where witchcraft is rampant. They work in every country
and society, changing the manner in which they work according to

each culture. They speak every language, have no sex and no color. But one thing is certain: wherever they are there is misery.

In Africa they cause poverty and disease (AIDS in particular at this moment), but in America they cause divorce and depression. America has the most powerful economy in the world; it is a land of unrivaled freedom and opportunity; it is a country where most people live in comfort, with money and everything else they need to be happy. And yet people are depressed. Why? People of other countries can't imagine Americans not being happy. But even though Americans enjoy prosperity and democracy, they suffer because they are not spiritually free.

Jesus Confronted Evil Spirits

Jesus' ministry was simple and straightforward: He taught and preached the Good News, healed the sick, and cast out demons. And because of this, He and His disciples affected people from every walk of life: prostitutes, military officers, fishermen, tax collectors, thieves, housewives, beggars, Pharisees, lepers, the blind, the crippled, and the demon possessed. Whatever people's problems were, Jesus had a clear and powerful solution, and He publicly demonstrated what God's will is for all who are suffering.

Reading the Gospels is so bracing and refreshing because it brings us back to what the true work of God ought to be. It is the power of God manifested through ordinary people, creating extraordinary results. This is the reason He sent the Holy Spirit, to equip us to carry on the work that He began. But healing and deliverance have become more of an exception than the rule in modern-day churches, and some who claim to practice it are unbiblical in their teachings and beliefs, causing many Christians to shy away from it.

Shying away from false teachers and insincere ministries is absolutely right, but shying away from the use of God's power to set the suffering free is not. When Jesus' disciples hesitated at times that faith was needed to transform lives, Jesus became upset with them. In one instance, a father brought his epileptic son to the disciples to be healed, but the disciples were unable to heal him. Jesus' reaction to their inability was: "O unbelieving generation… how long shall I stay with you? How long shall I put up with you?" (Mark 9:19). In another instance, Peter, while he was walking on the water, became afraid and sank. After Jesus had rescued him He said: "You of little faith...why did you doubt?" (Matthew 14:31) These responses clearly show His passionate desire to see the disciples walking in the mighty, unrivaled power of God. He couldn't bear to see people going through life being oppressed by problems and held back by demons when their faith had the power to break out of that oppressive existence and lead them into a new way of living.

Yet many Christians don't even believe that demons can still possess and oppress people today. Most who do believe think it only happens in very rare and unusual cases—which was not true in Jesus' ministry. If Jesus was grieved to see in people a lack of faith to cast out demons, how would He feel about Christians who don't even believe that demons still exist? It is precisely because of this lack of understanding of the devil and our power over him that we have problems that don't go away, even among long-time believers in the church.

Demon possession—an Old-fashioned Concept?

Paul says in his epistle to the Ephesians, "Put on the full armor of God, so that you will be able to stand firm against the schemes of the devil. For our struggle is not against flesh and blood, but against the rulers, against the powers, against the world forces of this darkness, against the spiritual forces of wickedness in the heavenly places" (Ephesians 6:11,12). Our struggle is a spiritual one. Those who are in the greatest suffering, who are lost and confused, who are prisoners to addictions, immorality, and violence, and who are oppressed by all kinds of evil will never be prayed for effectively if pastors and churches refuse to acknowledge the need for deliverance.

The work of Jesus and His disciples changed lives, without exception. By the Sea of Galilee, the Lord Jesus could deal with the legion of demons possessing a naked man, covered with scars from suicide attempts, who had torn apart iron chains and couldn't be restrained by anyone. And Jesus was able to deal just as comfortably with a hopelessly proud and religious rich young ruler. No one was too good or too bad for Him; He was ready and able to help every single person. If He is our Lord, we as His servants need to follow in His footsteps and do all we can to be a reflection of Him in this world. If churches are fearful of letting into their congregation undesirable people, who act strange and are clearly demonized, then they are nowhere near doing the work God called them to do. Attitudes have been changing within the last twenty to thirty years, and many have begun to realize that deliverance as seen in the Bible is as needed today as it was in the time of Jesus. But few churches are actually practicing it.

Never does the Bible give us any reason to think that demons would cease to exist or that casting them out would become unnecessary in the future (Romans 8:38; 1 Corinthians 10:20; James 2:19). The ministry of casting out demons, which the Lord Jesus began, is a powerful tool that He made available to us. If we choose to ignore this aspect of the ministry of the Church, the lives of people to whom we need to reach out will be destroyed unnecessarily and maybe even lost—and we ourselves run the risk of being deceived by demons by not developing the discernment and faith to fight against them.

The sheer number of biblical references proves the existence of evil spirits and our need to fight against them. There are a certain unchangeable facts of life on earth; one of them is the struggle between light and darkness, good and evil, God and the devil, angels and demons, truth and lies. We are not living in a perfect world. We are living in a world that tests our faith and forces us to choose between good and evil. We were not made as robots or puppets, going through predetermined movements. We are beings with the freedom to choose, and by that choice we demonstrate who we love: God or Satan. Though Satan and his demons are evil, they fulfill an important role in this earthly life that can't be ignored.

Is It Oppression from the Devil or a Test from God?

One question I've been frequently asked is, "How do I know when the devil is oppressing me and when I am just going through a test of the Lord?" First of all, we have to understand that no matter what the devil or his demons are trying to do to destroy our lives, God is far greater than all of them and will not permit them to do anything in our lives beyond what we can handle (1 Corinthians 10:13). Though they are rebellious, they still have to submit to Him and His plans. When sin is committed and a person's life is opened up to demonic attack, he will suffer the consequences of his actions. But though he has allowed the devil to enter his life, the suffering can become an opportunity for him to recognize how much he needs God and turn to the Lord in repentance. So, in that way, the attack of the devil and the plans of God overlap. God is so great He can take the worst problem and make it into a blessing.

Another pervasive attitude among American Christians is that suffering is a good and noble thing that we should embrace to purify our faith. Perhaps this comes from our Puritan roots. The book of James says, "Consider it all joy, my brethren, when you encounter various trials, knowing that the testing of your faith produces endurance" (James 1:2). It's a fantastic verse because it teaches us to look at our trials as a challenge to persevere in our faith. But faith in what? Faith that only when we die will we finally be released from this wretched life of suffering?

What the Holy Spirit is saying in James is far more positive and uplifting than that! The faith that God expects us to use is the faith that *fights back* against the evil trying to destroy our lives. It's the faith that our God is powerful and loving and good; He is the same God who healed the blind and deaf, raised the dead, and cast out demons. Counting it pure joy is an act of defiance against the devil, not just a passive acceptance of the problems. It takes a lot of faith to look at the destruction caused by the devil in our lives and laugh, knowing that our God will conquer in the end by our faith. The answers to our prayers are rarely instantaneous, but as we persevere in faith and joy, the evil that comes against us will have to collapse.

How do we know that we shouldn't just be patient and wait to be blessed in heaven after we die? Look at the continuation of this passage in verses 4-8:

> *"And let endurance have its perfect result, so that you may*
> *be perfect and complete, lacking in nothing. But if any of*
> *you lacks wisdom, let him ask of God, who gives to all gen-*
> *erously and without reproach, and it will be given to him.*

But he must ask in faith without any doubting, for the one who doubts is like the surf of the sea, driven and tossed by the wind. For that man ought not to expect that he will receive anything from the Lord, being a double-minded man, unstable in all his ways."

God's desire is for us to be mature and complete, not lacking in anything, right here on this earth. The process of maturing requires going through the hardships and battles that come our way and having an active and living faith to overcome. God doesn't just throw suffering in our face as a punishment to endure; He uses the burdens of this evil world as challenges for us to rise up and fight. But if we doubt, if we are wishy-washy in our faith, if we are passive or apathetic, we are useless to God and can be sure we won't receive anything from Him.

It's true that all our suffering will end when we reach heaven, and only there will our need to fight against temptations, weaknesses, doubts, and demonic attacks be finished forever. But these difficulties we face here on earth are meant to be defeated by His name and for His glory. If a believer who is suffering constant depression goes through therapy, prays, and reads the Bible but finds no relief, is he to just accept his debilitating condition and praise God for it? Apparently more than a few churches teach this, interpreting the passage in James in this hopeless way. But there is far more for us to be doing. God wants us to set people free from the captivity of the devil, and learning how to fight with faith and authority in the name of the Lord Jesus is where it all begins.

How Is Deliverance Possible?

It may be hard to understand how demons can still possess and oppress people as they did in Jesus' time. Looking at the Bible, some of the accounts of demon possession show people thrashing and convulsing, screaming, and even pulling apart iron chains. In this "modern" age, that kind of behavior is only seen in people with mental illnesses who are treated with sedation and therapy. And yet there are other examples in the Bible where people who seemed very normal had serious, incurable problems: for example, the mute and deaf epileptic and the woman bent double for eighteen years. There are people around us every single day who are suffering because of demonic attacks in their lives, and the only indications we have are the problems and fears that weigh these people down. But the devil still attacks people today as he did during the time of the Bible—just as God's power is still available, right now, for whoever desires to be set free.

When we pray to cast out demons from a person's life, we need to prayer with power and conviction, just as Jesus did. As we command evil spirits to manifest, they often do, speaking and thrashing just as the Bible describes. They make all sorts of horrible threats; I cannot count the number of times demons have told me they will kill their victim—me as well. I have seen kind and gentle people manifest demons that fight against me and other pastors, kicking and punching and wrestling against us until we command the demon to be tied up. I usually hold a manifesting demon behind the person's neck because I have seen demons try to smash their victim's head against the floor or walls, or try to throw them off the stage, or even try to run right out of the church and into oncoming traffic. But Jesus had authority over demons to drive them out; He passed that authority down to His disciples and to those of us who desire to give their lives completely to following Him.

Jesus has given us the authority to rebuke and cast out all demons, no matter what they have done and no matter how long they have been in the life of their victim. Inventing rituals and long intensive procedures to cast out demons is not at all the way Jesus and His disciples worked. Jesus' method was not complicated, and He treated the devil for what he was: a proud and evil fallen angel grasping for any kind of power because he knew his days were numbered. The devil and his demons make a lot of trouble and cause a lot of suffering, but compared to the awesome, majestic power of God, they are puny and defeated. This is the perspective that we need to have—if we have true faith in God. Without the sacrifice of Jesus we would be powerless before the devil, but because of His amazing grace, we are not only set free from sin and death, by His blood, but are made victorious over all evil that tries to destroy us in this world.

Jesus made it clear that demons do inhabit lives and that our job is to fight against them to rescue those stolen lives back. The terminology He uses is rough and aggressive: "...how can anyone enter a strong man's house and carry off his possessions unless he first ties up the strong man? Then he can rob his house" (Matthew 12:29 NIV). Jesus could have used other metaphors for the process of casting out demons, but he chose violent ones for a reason. We as Christians need to be ruthless against the devil. We need to understand our authority in Jesus, come against the "strong man" with no fear or trepidation, tie him up, and throw him out so we can "rob" all that he stole from us. This is generally not the attitude of the typical American Christian, but it was definitely the attitude of the Lord Jesus. If we are His followers, we need to get in line with His Spirit and start aggressively attacking our enemies.

> *"Now when the unclean spirit goes out of a man, it passes through waterless places seeking rest, and does not find it. Then it says, 'I will return to my house from which I came'; and when it comes it finds it unoccupied, swept, and put in order. Then it goes and takes along with it seven other spirits more wicked that itself, and they go in and live there; and the last state of that man becomes worse than the first. That is the way it will also be with this evil generation"* (Matthew 12:43-45).

Evil spirits are at rest when they are living in a person's body; when they can't find a life to occupy, they are constantly wandering in arid, lifeless places. Jesus explains the way demons think after being cast out of someone's life: "I will return to my house from which I came." He reveals that our physical bodies are potential houses in which the demons might live—we are all targets because they cannot find rest without occupying one of our bodies. But at the same time, God is waiting for us to open our hearts in humble submission to Him so that we can be transformed into the temple of the Holy Spirit, where evil spirits have no way to enter. The apostle Paul writes, "Don't you know that you yourselves are God's temple and that God's Spirit lives in you?" (1 Corinthians 3:16). Whether we realize it or not, we're in the middle of an unending spiritual struggle. Evil spirits crave the use of our minds and bodies to cause all sorts of misery and destruction; at the same time, the Holy Spirit longs to live in us, bring us abundant life, and transform us into the likeness of Jesus Christ (see John 14:23).

Matthew 12 reveals that evil spirits come to live in a person's body just like people would live in a house. Without a body to live in these spirits are homeless, wandering from here to there. They "pass through waterless places seeking rest," as if they were in a desert without food, water, or any life-giving sustenance. From this we can deduce that since living in a person's body gives demons rest, nourishment, drink, and everything else that's needed to grow and thrive, then our suffering, sickness, grudges, hatred, fears, addictions, and doubts are the food and drink of demons.

Evil spirits can only enter a person whose body ("house") is unoccupied. The demons were able to return to the house in Jesus' example because it was swept clean and put in order but not occupied by anyone. Since Jesus had not been invited in and given ownership of that house, demons were free to return and make things even worse than before. Cleaning up the house was Jesus' analogy for casting out the spirits that were there before. Putting everything in order is the same as getting rid of our sinful habits—smoking, drinking, living in immorality, treating others with selfishness, etc. But Jesus is showing that this is not enough; we have to allow the Holy Spirit to come and take control of our hearts, occupy our house. Our life can't just be clean, it has to be filled with the presence of God. Otherwise, we become an open target for demons to attack us again.

This is such a simple concept, but many Christians are confused when they see other believers falling into terrible sins or suffering unending attacks. New converts in our churches are a cause for great rejoicing, but just because they have chosen to give up their past does not mean that their battle is over. I've heard innumerable testimonies from people who, crying in humility before the church, claimed to be free from addictions. But, as months passed, they were back in their old way of life. There are others, however, who came from horrible pasts, who seemed beyond help, who have found freedom and grown in the power of God for years and years. Some of them are even pastors and prayer counselors now, able to give strength and faith to those who suffer the same problems as they had years before.

The difference between those who found lasting freedom and those who didn't is the level of dedication they had in seeking the presence of God in their lives. They had to go beyond the miracle of healing or deliverance that God so graciously gave to them and humble themselves even more to give Him complete ownership of their lives. This didn't come from just a prayer during an altar call, but from a deep, ongoing conviction within their hearts—from a desire to be truly born again.

How Much Power Do Demons Have?

There has always been an air of mystery and fear about evil spirits. When people around Jesus saw Him cast out demons they reacted in amazement, asking each other where He had gotten such authority and power. Not only that, many accepted this act of casting out demons as proof that He was the Messiah, the Christ. Even Jesus showed how right these reactions were when He said, "But if I drive out demons by the Spirit of God, then the kingdom of God has come upon you" (Matthew 12:28). But today, as in practically every age, people react in fear to the subject of demons. If churches do accept the idea that deliverance is a real issue, they generally relegate these types of problems to "deliverance ministries," which are marveled at for their courage to accept such a strange and dangerous calling.

Yet this attitude of shying away from demons is completely foreign to the Bible. Driving out evil spirits was a very common part of a day's work for the Lord Jesus and His disciples—something simple, frequently performed in public, and powerful. In the ninth chapter of Matthew it says:

> "As they were going out, a mute, demon-possessed man
> was brought to Him. After the demon was cast out, the
> mute man spoke; and the crowds were amazed, and were
> saying, 'Nothing like this has ever been seen in Israel'"
> (Matthew 9:32,33).

There was no "deliverance team" with one person taking notes, another speaking in tongues, and another reading the Bible while Jesus ordered the evil spirit to leave (this is what many deliverance ministries advise today). There were no questionnaires or long, involved interviews. Jesus didn't give them reading assignments and a future "deliverance appointment" before casting out the demons. He simply used His authority, right then and there, and sent it away. It was also done in public—respectfully, but nonetheless in public—with the purpose of opening people's eyes to the fact that invisible evil forces actually do exist and that those who use their faith in Him can overcome them. All this seems to be very different from the way deliverance is carried out today.

How often do people react to the gospel by being amazed and saying, like the crowd with Jesus, "Nothing like this has ever been seen"? Isn't this what we want and need? Aren't Christians longing to have unbelievers react to the Word of God in such a way?

I remember the day in 1987 when Evelyn and I, for the first time, saw evil spirits manifesting in a church in Rio de Janeiro, Brazil. I will never forget how the pastor treated it as something common and completely under control. The manifesting spirits were screaming and thrashing around, making all sorts of horrible threats and speaking about what they had done in the lives of the people they were destroying. The pastor simply humiliated the demons in front of the entire congregation—by forcing them to confess their defeat before the Lord Jesus—and then cast them out! I was trembling the entire time. I had never seen the power of the devil manifested in such a way, and I had never seen the power of God made so real and clear. The difference in the people who went through deliverance was like night and day, and it instantly deepened my love for God, giving me an assurance of His great power to answer us when we cry out to Him. More than that, it was a wake-up call for me; there is a great spiritual war going on around us every day, and if we don't learn how to fight, we're bound to get hurt.

When demons come in contact with Christians who know both their position before God and the authority they have in Jesus Christ, the evil spirits are simply outmatched. Yet if we want to defeat the spiritual forces of darkness, it is vital for us to be clear in our understanding of them. We do have power over them in the name of Jesus, and like the disciples came back from various towns and cities rejoicing that even the demons obeyed them, we can have that same experience if we put our faith into practice. (Of course, as Jesus taught them, our rejoicing should be, first and foremost, that we have received His salvation by grace.)

Though demons claim certain people as "theirs," no one is the permanent possession of evil spirits; the sacrifice of Jesus does away with the separation between man and God. Though demons may live within a person, they do not have the power to take away that person's free will. Each person has the ability to reach out for God's help and to reject the evil that's in their life, even if it's just a desire in their hearts. They may not have the strength to simply walk away from their sinful life, but they can begin to change their attitudes and cry out to God. No matter how many demons are working—or how deeply they have taken root in someone's life—there is always hope for change through the Lord Jesus. As long as we are alive on earth, we have the freedom to choose life or death, Jesus or the devil.

Can Demons Work in Christians?

It is surprising to many people that an evil spirit manifested in Ann, a faithful church member who believed in God and was trying her best to be a good Christian. It's common for believers to assume that as soon as a person repents and prays the sinner's prayer that the devil is, from that moment on, unable to work in his life. But the subject of how the devil works and whom he can attack is much deeper than this. Ann's faithful church attendance and desire to follow Jesus cannot be denied, but neither can her terrible nightmares, insomnia, visions of the dead, and bad habits. We are forced to admit the possibility of possessed believers: people who believe in the Lord Jesus Christ but struggle with ongoing sins, addictions, or serious, debilitating problems that resist all normal attempts at resolution.

Jesus' words in Matthew make perfect sense in this situation: "You will know them by their fruits. Grapes are not gathered from thorn bushes nor figs from thistles, are they? So every good tree bears good fruit, but the bad tree bears bad fruit" (Matthew 7:16,17). In my experience, this verse has been almost completely ignored by certain Christians and church leaders who have taken things for granted instead of looking for the proof of a changed life. If we are spiritually free, there will be good fruit to confirm our freedom—just as there will be bad fruit to confirm oppression or possession by evil spirits. Our character and life reveal who is living inside our hearts: Jesus or the devil.

We've got to realize that demons are terrorists. They don't play by any rules. They are ruthless. If the people of God rise up and take a stand, demons are forced into submission. But if no one stands in their way they will attack anyone, regardless of who they are or what they've done to deserve the attack. They'll inhabit innocent children and unborn babies, those who are vulnerable in any way or dealing with trauma or abuse. Young or old, rich or poor, they don't care who they destroy, as long as it is a human life.

Unlike the Lord Jesus, who is knocking at the door of our hearts and waiting for us to open so He can come inside (Revelation 3:20), demons sneak under the door, crawl through a crack in the window or force their way in however they can. They are criminals, liars, deceivers, trespassers; they promise their followers the world and then stab them in the back without giving them a thing. No matter what's right or just, whether a person is good or bad, spirits of darkness want just one thing: to spread fear and destruction as far and as wide as possible.

Since the 9/11 attacks, our government has taken steps to protect our country based on the conviction that terrorists respond to nothing but force. As Christians we know that, in our personal lives, love and kindness has to underscore our behavior and character towards others. But towards the devil and his demons we have to be utterly ruthless—either we counterattack with all our strength, or we get run over!

"From the days of John the Baptist until now, the kingdom of heaven has been forcefully advancing, and forceful men lay hold of it" (Matthew 11:12 NIV).

CHAPTER THREE

Twelve Signs of Possession or Oppression

Determining whether or not a person has demons at work in his life is not as difficult as it may seem. Although some ministries go through lengthy interviews and examine every detail of a person's life before venturing to cast out any demons, the Bible never alludes to any similar procedure. Jesus cast out demons every day, and He didn't spend too much time talking about the finer points of deliverance. He very bluntly said that the thief comes to kill, steal, and destroy, and when we see destruction, especially a type of destruction that seems to have no solution, in our lives or those around us, we can be sure that demons are present.

This doesn't mean that we can ignore our own responsibility to do what is right—we can't play the game of "the devil made me do it." Demons work in conjunction with our own sinful behavior and our love of the things of this world. On the other hand, it is naive to imagine that we can simply change the horrible problems in our lives by a mere decision to be good. When we see the signs of a demon's presence, acknowledging that he is inside of us should force us to have an even greater sense of responsibility to drive it out—and change whatever is necessary in our attitudes and behavior to keep it out.

Although the devil is ultimately the one responsible for all evil, sickness, and unhappiness, not all problems are due to demon possession. But possession itself is apparent when ordinary solutions just don't work any more. If a disease is beyond the help of treatments, it is more than just a disease; it has a spirit at work behind it to make it incurable. Addictions may be reigned in through therapy and constant vigilance, but a person can only truly return to a normal life when the demons of addiction are cast out. Uncontrollable desires, fears, incurable diseases, and evil supernatural experiences are clear signs of demonic oppression or possession.

A doctor arrives at a diagnosis of his patient's disease by identifying the symptoms. When a farmer walks through an orchard he knows the trees by the fruit hanging from the branches. Every disease has its symptoms, and every tree has its fruits. The same is true when evil spirits inhabit a person's body; signs appear that would not appear in a person who is free, a person whose life is filled with the Spirit of God. This understanding is confirmed over and over again by the Lord Jesus when he compared people's lives to good or bad trees (Matthew 3:10; 7:17; 12:33; Luke 3:9; John 15:1-8).

His teaching on this subject is amazingly simple. He said:

> "*For there is no good tree which produces bad fruit, nor, on the other hand, a bad tree which produces good fruit. For each tree is known by its own fruit. For men do not gather figs from thorns, nor do they pick grapes from a briar bush. The good man out of the good treasure of his heart brings forth what is good; and the evil man out of the evil treasure brings forth what is evil; for his mouth speaks from that which fills his heart*" (Luke 6:43-45).

Certain bad habits or problems cannot just be passed off as, "Well, I'm only human. Everybody makes mistakes." That's very true, but the type and severity of a problem we have reveals what is in our hearts. Our problems are like a litmus or a TB test, revealing things we don't see with our eyes.

The following list describes how evil spirits work and what signs indicate their presence. As you will notice, they are symptoms that many people suffer from—people around us who are apparently normal, our friends, family, and co-workers. The Hollywood image of a demon-possessed person being a mentally deranged monster could not be farther from the truth. Evil spirits victimize people from all walks of life. It's important to note that though being oppressed by demonic spirits is sometimes due to the willful, conscious sin of a person, there are many people who are suffering this kind of attack who have no idea that they were open targets.

1. Fits of Rage

This is a very common manner in which evil spirits work, making people extremely sensitive and easily irritated to the point that they suddenly explode in fits of uncontrolled, violent anger. There's no lack of examples of this in the news today. In fact, it seems to be much more common than ever before. There are the latest large-scale examples of genocide: in Rwanda, where millions were senselessly slaughtered; and Bosnia, where ethnic cleansing caused unimaginable suffering and pain. There are also incidents, closer to home, of school killings like the tragedy at Columbine. And there are the daily occurences of murder and abuse that every single community goes through. Other incidents are also on the rise, such as, road rage, sexual abuse in the family, parents killing or maiming their own children—it seems that anything is possible these days.

Many of these tragedies cannot be explained in normal ways. We find ourselves wondering how people could reached such heights of unbridled rage, and we are left confused and shaking our heads. But when we realize that evil spirits can enter and attack the nervous system of a person, many times making their home there, the source of all the violence around us becomes apparent.

2. Constant Headaches

Demons use every kind of sicknesses to oppress people, but constant headaches are so common that they deserve special attention.

(I've devoted an entire chapter to this subject; see Chapter 7.) There is no mention of migraines in the Bible; it's something we have noticed from years of praying for people around the world. Constant headaches and pains that do not respond to aspirin or Tylenol, or even to the treatments of doctors, are clearly demonic. Not only do these headaches cause terrible pains, but they greatly interfere with a person's job. They create confusion and exhaustion, situations in which demons thrive (see Job 2:7).

My mother constantly suffered from headaches. She was a strong Christian who was always helping and encouraging others in their faith, but for most of her life she was oppressed with terrible migraines. They kept her up at night and, when they were extremely bad, kept her in bed during the day—even though she hated to be held back in any way and would force herself to go about her normal activities even when she was in terrible pain. Yet, even so, it affected her life, marriage, and children in a profound way.

3. Insomnia

This is nothing more than an extension of fear and worry manifesting itself in a debilitating way. Frequently, this is one of the first tools of the devil. I'm not talking about sleeplessness for a night because you're in anxious anticipation about your new job or school—that's a normal part of life. But severe insomnia—the kind that lasts for months, even years, the kind that doesn't end—is a form of demonic oppression or possession. I've spoken to people who haven't slept in years because of pain, fear, worries, or even visions and nightmares.

How can this be demonic? Sleep is as necessary to the body as food and water, and the lack of it is slow death of body, mind, and spirit. When you are exhausted, the pleasure of life is drained away, you lose your ability to concentrate, you are not careful with your responsibilities, and your health deteriorates day by day. By robbing you of sleep, the devil's job of stealing, killing, and destroying becomes much, much easier. On the other hand, a person who trusts in God is protected from these attacks and is able to sleep well, even in the worst times, because he has the assurance that God is in control (see Psalm 127:2; Proverbs 3:24).

It's amazing how many people come to the church who haven't slept properly in years! Many do not sleep at all, and I sometimes wonder how they can function. There was a man who had lived with this problem for more than seven years after getting involved with Gypsies and their spells. Once he had gone into a church somewhere in Europe and asked a pastor to pray for him. Suddenly, in the middle of the prayer, both fell over backwards. All the blood drained from the pastor's face and, trembling, he told the man never to step foot in his church again. "I have a wife and children that I love, I can't afford to get mixed up in the curses that are on you. Find someone else to pray for you. I can't ever pray for you again." For years afterward the man's suffering continued to increase. When he came to us, we prayed for him and he manifested violently, throwing my father against the wall. After taking authority over the demon, my father cast it out, and the man went home and slept for thirty-six hours straight—without eating, going to the bathroom, or even moving. He slept so soundly that his girlfriend kept checking to see if he was still alive. But from that time on his insomnia disappeared—as well as other serious problems in his health and love life—and he began to enjoy life like never before.

4. Incurable diseases

Like the ailments of the deaf-mute epileptic and the daughter of Abraham bent over for eighteen years, there are sicknesses that have no medical cure—not because technology hasn't advanced that far, but because the cause is beyond the realm of the medical profession. I would say that there are two types of sicknesses caused by demons: there is the demon that hides behind a genuine sickness, exaggerating the symptoms and impeding its cure; and there is the demon that uses no particular disease but produces all kinds of terrible symptoms that make no sense whatsoever to doctors. The first sickness can be diagnosed by a doctor with tests and exams, although its severity and unresponsive nature remain a mystery; the second one is just plain non-diagnosable.

5. Fear

It's no wonder that modern psychology has so many terms for fear. There's a phobia for almost any situation you can imagine.

Unfortunately, we do not just see this among unbelievers only, but among believers as well.

Fear can disguise itself as a sense of responsibility and concern for problems that might happen in the future if not prevented, but in truth fear is more than just concern; it's a deception of the devil sent to convince people that God is powerless and that prayer is hopeless. Ordinary people that hold down jobs and take care of homes can be carrying this spirit with them, a spirit that will eventually suffocate their lives.

Fear is the opposite of faith. Faith says, "Everything looks terrible, and, by all logical accounts, I should prepare for the worst—but because the Lord is my God, He is going to do the impossible and make a way for me." Faith *forces* the obstacles to move. Faith always believes in the best to come, not because it is irrational, but because it knows God intimately. Fear, on the other hand, is pathetically whiny and weak! It says, "Everything looks terrible, I should prepare for the worst—and there is absolutely nothing I or anyone can do to get me out of this. Life is terrible; it's time to panic!" Having fear is the same as denying God.

The Bible talks about fear throughout the Old and New Testaments. The phrase, "Do not be afraid," appears commonly. Psalm 23 speaks of having no fear. The apostle John writes: "There is no fear in love. But perfect love drives out fear" (1 John 4:18). In other words, when we are in a close and loving relationship with God and our lives are right before Him, fear has no place; it is driven out by the love that we experience from Him. We can conclude that the presence of fear can only mean the absence of communion with God—an empty house, a target for wandering demons to possess (see Luke 12:4-7,22-34).

6. Seizures

In the Bible, the young man whose father brought him to Jesus to be healed is an example of someone with this evil spirit. We see this constantly in the church: people tell us that they cannot function because of uncontrollable seizures. I remember one woman in South Africa who commonly would have a seizure while she was crossing the street or walking down the sidewalk. At times people would stop to help, but at other times no one would stop and she would be left to roll around on the ground until the seizure left. Sometimes she'd be doused with a bucket of cold water. When she would come to, she would be dirty, cut, and bruised—and having come dangerously close to being run over by cars. She told me that the seizures would come at the worst moments: when she was going for a job interview; when she was at a bus stop; or when she was crossing a busy street. We prayed for her, casting out the evil spirits, and this woman was healed of all seizures. She never suffered from them again. This has happened to many other people who've come to the church.

7. Suicidal Thoughts

King's Saul is an example from the Old Testament of someone who was tormented by suicidal thoughts. Saul had become rebellious towards God and was intent on killing David out of jealousy. He visited a witch and finally committed suicide rather than allow his enemies to capture him (1 Samuel 15:1-9; 16:14,15; 18:10-16; 28:7-25; 31:4). Saul had clearly become demonized.

Judas Iscariot is another example. He was one of the twelve apostles, he had cast out demons and healed the sick, yet was a thief and greedy for money. Jesus called him a devil, and Judas hanged himself rather than confess his sin and humble himself. Without a doubt, he was demon possessed (see Mathew 10:4; 26:15; 27:5; Luke 9:1-6; 22:3; John 12:6).

Thoughts of suicide come in moments of extreme despair and hopelessness, when people feel that no one can help, that they are all alone. Yet these feelings and thoughts are lies from the mouth of Satan and his demons. There is no reason for us to despair in a world where God is in control. A study note in the Nelson Study Bible says:

> "'I will never leave you nor forsake you': This quotation is one of the most emphatic statements in the New Testament. In Greek it contains two double negatives, similar to saying in English, 'I will never, ever, ever forsake you.' Jesus uses the same technique to express the certainty of eternal life for believers (see John 10:28)."[1]

Though not every person who has suicidal thoughts knows the Bible, there is an innate knowledge in all of us that God exists and is powerful and good, just as Romans 1:20 says. Even for those who have never heard the teachings of the gospel or known the name of Jesus Christ, their sense of self-preservation and love for their own life is a natural, God-given instinct. And beyond this instinct is the conviction of God's love and the peace that comes when a person has Jesus *occupying* his heart and mind. The presence of God sets a believer worlds away from despair and hopelessness. Suicidal thoughts are demonic in nature because they go against the very nature of God and everything that He teaches in His Word (Hebrews 13:5; John 10:28; 1 Corinthians 10:13). God loved us so much that He gave His Son Jesus to forgive our sins and empower us to be overcomers in this world.

People with suicidal thoughts need a great deal of love and compassion. They are victims of demonic lies, but they should not be condemned as evil people just because they have lost the will to live. Through strong prayers of deliverance, practical counseling, care, and support, their attacks can be overcome and their lives set free.

8. Depression

The dictionary describes depression as "a psychoneurotic or psychotic disorder marked especially by sadness, inactivity, difficulty in thinking and concentration, a significant increase or decrease in appetite and time spent sleeping, feelings of dejection and hopelessness, and sometimes suicidal tendencies.[2] Of course, depression can be a psychological or psychiatric problem that can be helped with specialized treatment and medications, but only superficially. By looking at this definition, we can see that demons use many or all of these symptoms, which are caused by a deep conviction that either God does not exist or that He does not care. Depression, in short, is a rejection of God's truth. When it's only treated medically the root of the problem will never be removed. There are people who've spent their entire adult lives on medication, unable to function normally, because the underlying spirit of depression and sadness occupies their mind and heart.

9. Addictions

The harmfulness of an addiction to nicotine, alcohol, or drugs lies not just in its physiological affects to the body, but also in its affect to the character and morality of a person. Self-control is abandoned and a mind-altered state is entered into, and it is specifically this aspect of an addiction that opens the way for demons to control us. The less self-control we have over our fleshly nature the more demons can work, and in a mind-altered state they are free to do whatever they want (Romans 13:13; Galatians 5:21; 1 Peter 4:3). Cigarettes might not lead to a mind-altering state, but they reveal a dependence on something other than God. Cigarettes can also be a steppingstone to other addictions. It's interesting to note that when people get drunk or high they normally start to chain smoke; this shows that there is a definite connection.

10. An Unstable Love Life

Marriage and family are two of the greatest enemies of the devil. Because God loves marriage and considers it holy, Satan works hard to destroy it in every way he can. The abundance of pornography, R- and X-rated films, and seductive photographs (sprinkling even fairly straight-laced magazines) are testaments to this, as are the current divorce rates all over the world. TV shows draw audiences with crude comedy and suggestive situations. When a person has abnormal problems finding a good man or woman to marry or has recurrent irresolvable misunderstandings in his love life, many times this is caused by an evil spirit. This spirit often is sent with the specific mission of destroying that person's future marriage or ensuring that he will never be happy in marriage.

Marriage is so important to God that it is compared to the relationship between Jesus Christ and the Church (Ephesians 5:22-33). Though there are some people who never feel the need for a partner, most people have a deep-seated need for this type of relationship. When they're unable to get married, they fall into profound depression and loneliness because of their unfulfilled needs. Of course, sexual promiscuity, homosexuality, and perversions of all types are signs of demon possession as well. The Word of God tells us that the sexual relationship has a spiritual dimension that bonds a couple together, making them one flesh. When that holy and spiritual bond is abused and defiled, it becomes demonic. In the Old Testament these types of behavior were to be punished by death, showing us how abominable they are in the eyes of God.

Divorce is another issue here. I'm not saying that all divorced people are demonized, but divorce and broken homes are clearly caused by the devil; he uses our own failures and unresolved issues to destroy families. Although some marriages cannot be saved, such as when one of the partners is absolutely unwilling to change, most can be saved if even one side turns to God and asks for His power to deliver them from the hands of the devil. There are plenty of divorced Christians who thought they had done all they could do but never knew how to fight against the spiritual forces that were ripping their marriage apart.

11. Hearing Voices and Seeing Visions

Anyone who has counseled those who are demon possessed knows how frequently demons use dreams, visions, and prophesies. One example is the demonized slave woman that Paul set free:

> *"It happened that as we were going to the place of prayer, a slave-girl having a spirit of divination met us, who was bringing her masters much profit by fortune-telling. Following after Paul and us, she kept crying out, saying, 'These men are bond-servants of the Most High God, who are proclaiming to you the very way of salvation.' She continued doing this for many days. But Paul was greatly annoyed, and turned and said to the spirit, 'I command you in the name of Jesus Christ to come out of her!' And it came out at that very moment"* (Acts 16:16-18).

Demons use mystical powers such as fortune-telling, prophecy, visions, dreams, and the interpreting of dreams to attract people, then they use these very same means to deceive and destroy them. I've counseled countless people who've come to me saying that they dream about the future—simple ordinary things mostly, but at times terrible accidents. When they actually see with their own eyes what they dreamed the night before, they become convinced that they have a "gift" and that they really do receive revelations about the future. The next step, then, is for them to start basing decisions on their dreams. Sometimes these people don't even want to sleep at night because they dread knowing what terrible things will happen the next morning. At other times demons cause people to have visions of relatives, Jesus, the devil, or strange creatures that cause either elation or terror in the victims. Other times fortune-tellers and mediums that prophesy, like the slave girl in the above passage, are used by demons—even revealing true personal facts about a person's life.

These things should be no mystery to us. Every one of the above experiences is a trick designed to attract innocent, curious victims to the kingdom of darkness. To deceive a potential believer, demons will gladly join together, share information, or even agree to cause certain accidents the next morning. It's important to remember that the devil has power as well as God, though his power cannot be compared to that of God. But the simple fact that certain experiences involve supernatural power does not mean that they are good for us or that they are from God (see Matthew 7:21-23; Mark 13:22; 2 Thessalonians 2:9,10).

12. Involvement in Witchcraft and the Occult

This is an obvious sign that many Christians accept as demonic, although surprisingly few would know how to deal with a witch walking into their church and asking for help! Although people involved in the occult like to imagine that they do only "good magic" and are nothing like Satanists, the Bible shows us that they are all one and the same. Communication with any spirit that is not the Spirit of God is demonic and an open invitation to the devil to enter a person's life.

Conclusion

This list is in no way an exhaustive one, but it is meant to give a basic idea of how demons can be seen in people's lives. The devil manifests himself in many forms, and God has given us His Word and His Spirit to help us discern what spirits are at work around us.

Maybe these signs seem too commonplace to be considered demonic, but it's time to look at our lives, and the lives of those we love, through the eyes of God rather than those of society. If it seems too radical to imagine that our kindhearted neighbor may be demon possessed, just remember, it is radical! It's right in line with the radical way of thought that Jesus introduced to the world when He began His ministry. Although those who are demon possessed have their own part to play in finding deliverance, they are not necessarily evil people nor should we blame them for the existence of demons in their lives. Many are victims who found themselves under attack and did not understand what was going on or how to react with faith. Things are not always as they first appear, and the devil is not eager to be discovered. Unmasking the presence of demons is the beginning of the process to cast them out and find true freedom in Christ.

CHAPTER FOUR

How Do Evil Spirits Enter a Person?

"People were actually betting on who would be the next to die in our family," Eva said in the pre-interview for our TV program in Los Angeles. It sounded so extreme that I wondered if it was an exaggeration. But as she continued, I realized that death was no stranger to her family. Her mother, brother, and sister had all died of Huntington's Chorea, an inherited disease that develops in adults and leads to dementia, a loss of coordination, and, eventually, death.

"I grew up expecting to lose my mind and die around the age of forty. I never expected to have a long, happy life because this disease was in my blood. Drugs, alcohol, and parties were a way of life for everyone in my family; I had no idea there was any other way of coping. There was no real right or wrong for us, only what felt good at the time. We were always sad to see family members in prison, but we just accepted it as a normal part of life for us—like so many families who lived in our neighborhood.

"At twenty-six I tried crack and was hooked for six months straight! That's all I did. I didn't sleep; I didn't even care about my baby girl. I smoked crack twenty-four hours a day. I left my job, smoked my entire three-thousand-dollar tax refund, sold my car everything in my house for more crack, and eventually lost my house. Then I moved in with a dope dealer and became her slave for more drugs. My father ended up taking my daughter away from me because all I cared about was my addiction.

"A strange thing happened while I was smoking crack. I began to hear voices, like an invisible person was talking to me, which is what I thought it was at first. But later I realized no one was there and no one else heard what I heard. It became clear that they were demonic voices. They would constantly say bad things about me. I heard them speaking about how they were going to kill me, to kill those around me. Whenever I tried to have thoughts about a happy family, success, or health, the voices would immediately start tearing me down and saying the opposite, making me really scared and confused."

Eva finally found her freedom at Living Faith, through a process of prayers of deliverance and learning how to live a life of faith and submission to the Lord. The voices have stopped, as well as the fear and oppression that came with her addictions. She has no trace of Huntington's Chorea, and she is healthy and strong. She now runs her own day care facility and is seeing more and more of God's blessing in her life. Although she had many openings in her past to allow the devil to attack her, God's grace through the sacrifice of Jesus on the cross has given her the power to overcome the worst problems and put her old life behind her.

Open Doors

Involvement in the occult and Satanism is a very obvious invitation for evil spirits to inhabit our lives, yet there are many other sins and weaknesses that unlock our hearts and minds to their work. From the Bible we know that something is demonic if it encourages a person to worship anything or anyone other than the God of the Bible or if it causes us to be rebellious towards Him. The following pages contain a list of some common attitudes or actions that allow demons to enter our lives. This is not a complete list—I'm sure there is more that could be added to it—but hopefully it will be helpful as a rough guide.

Most of the actions that allow demons into our lives overlap with the signs of demon possession, like in the cases of addictions, fear, anger, and immorality that we studied in Chapter 3. As sins are committed (sometimes only once is enough), the spirit that accompanies that sin enters a person and can torment and enslave. It's popular among the psychiatric professions, and others who study human behavior, to blame genetics or brain development for certain kinds of habits or emotional states. Although it may be true that CT scans and other tests can identify hormonal or chemical changes in a person's body according to their psychological state, just altering body chemicals with drug treatments does not affect the spirit behind the problem. A common pattern evident among people who come from abusive families is the cycle of violence in which they are trapped. Though they hate the abuse they suffered as children, many turn around and abuse their own children in one way or another— a horrifying example of how demonic forces have a hunger to destroy whatever is pure and innocent and how spirits can be carried on from generation to generation (which will be discussed more in the next section).

People are quick to explain that they are the way they are simply because of their unique personality, almost glorifying their spiritual weakness as if it were a virtue. Psychiatry and studies on human behavior can only observe actions and thoughts, but they don't have the depth of spiritual understanding to recognize the presence of evil spirits. The Word of God has to show us how He expects us to live. The fruit of the Spirit is our standard, and whatever comes from the fruit of our flesh is not just from ourselves, but from the darkness (Galatians 5:16-25).

I have learned, along with the pastors and bishops with whom I've worked, that demons have certain consistent tendencies wherever they many be found around the world. After counseling and praying for thousands upon thousands of people, many of whom were demonized, we have heard manifesting demons speak and explain their work and have learned some things about how they operate and enter into minds and hearts.

Evil spirits are liars. But that doesn't mean that they never tell the truth. In the Bible, Jesus asked demons for information and they answered in obedience. As a rule, whenever manifesting spirits speak we need to use the gift of discernment to distinguish what is the truth and what is a lie. I wouldn't want anyone to think that manifesting spirits are to be treated with any sort of respect, but it's a fact that when Jesus cast out demons He sometimes allowed them to talk. In the instance of the man in the region of the Garasenes Jesus asked the demon his name (see Mark 5:1-20). When the demons answered, the Bible records their answer and Jesus does not challenge it— meaning that it was indeed the name of that group of demons. Other times Jesus commanded demons to be quiet, not because they were lying but because they were declaring the truth at a time when Jesus didn't want to advertise His real identity. In Mark it says, "Whenever the evil spirits saw Him, they fell down before Him and cried out, 'You are the Son of God.' But He gave them strict orders not to tell who He was" (Mark 3:11,12). So, when I say that we've learned from experience how demons work, you should understand that in fact it is possible to gain truthful facts from evil spirits.

Inherited Demons—the Generational Curse

When asked how long he's been in a person's life, many times a demon will respond, "Since he was in his mother's womb." We soon discover that the same demonic manifestation—the same addiction, the same unbridled temper, the same inability to have a happy marriage, etc.—exist in both parent and child. In some instances, every family member has had the same failures or diseases as far back as you can look into that person's family. Sometimes the problems attack every man in the family, other times only the women. Someone in the past opened the door for demons to enter—through witchcraft, idolatry, addictions, fears or worries—and once inside one member of the family, the demons consider that family their possession.

Countless times I have heard manifesting spirits declare, as we ordered them out, "She's mine! I'll never leave!" Of course, in the end they have to leave in the name of Jesus, but their attitude was very clear: they were convinced that they owned that person or the entire family. And many times I have found that the person suffering from attacks is not responsible for the demons entering his life. Because a relative in the past had opened a door for the devil, demons were able to infiltrate the entire family. Unless someone stands up and takes authority over the evil spirits in the name of Jesus, they'll continue to work in that family forever.

In the formation of the laws in the Old Testament, God punished those who committed sin and idolatry by punishing them and their descendants after them. But in the book of Ezekiel, God speaks to his people, who are looking forward to the coming of their Messiah, that a day would come where each man would be judged according to his own sins and not bear the punishment of his father. Now, as we live under the law of the Spirit, God either rewards us or disciplines us according to our own actions, but Satan, as we said before, finds any way to enter a life to destroy it whether it be through the sins or weaknesses of individuals, or through their family line.

"You shall not worship them or serve them; for I, the Lord your God, am a jealous God, visiting the iniquity of the fathers on the children on the third and fourth generations of those who hate Me, but showing lovingkindness to thousands, to those who love Me and keep My commandments" (Exodus 20:5-6).

Monica

In 1993, I met a young lady in Soweto, South Africa, named Monica Ngobane. She was carried into our church in Johannesburg, which was in the basement of a large office building, with open sores all over her body. She smelled terrible, couldn't walk or bathe herself, and had blood and infectious liquids oozing out of her wounds; for years she had barely been able to sleep at night because of the unbearable pain. Every morning the sheets that she had slept on would have to be peeled away from the wounds and washed because they were drenched with the infection. During the day, flies covered many of her wounds, infesting them with maggots that fed off of her raw flesh.

After many consultations, treatments, and tests, the doctors were unable to discover the cause and recommended that both of her legs be amputated at the knee. After this diagnosis, she began visiting spiritual healers and witchdoctors, as is common practice in South Africa. For the next couple of years she continued to get worse, yet she always hoped that she would find someone with a solution. After four years of this disease her family became sick of caring for her as an invalid and spending money for nothing. She was convinced that this sickness would kill her because she had seen both her aunt and cousin die from the same disease. Each one had suffered from it for four years, and she was sure her time was up.

By the grace of God Monica heard about the many miracles that happened in our church, and she came to seek God's help. During the prayers for healing and deliverance, she manifested evil spirits and felt a presence leave her body as it was cast out. That night an enormous change happened. Her wounds began to drain heavily, and the pain began to fade away. Within three weeks of faithfully coming to church for prayer, those open wounds closed up, and she could walk normally again. As I write this, she's been healed and free for ten years. She recently married a faithful Christian man in the church, and she is the manager of an upscale men's clothing store in Rosebank, Johannesburg. Best of all, her faith and devotion to the Lord Jesus Christ is firm and unwavering.

Monica was the victim of demons that were inherited in some way, demons that were being passed down from generation to generation. With the help of pastors in the church, she broke the power of these spirits through the name of Jesus, and now her family is free from that particular problem. No one in the past ten years has come down with the disease.

Witchcraft

Involvement in witchcraft, the occult, and Satanism is clearly against everything that is taught in the Bible and a sure way to become demon possessed. After working for sixteen years among many people from the West Indies and countries all over Africa, I have seen the affects of witchcraft on thousands of people's lives, and I have seen thousands set free from these demons. As I mentioned in Chapter 3, some forms of witchcraft, such as Wicca, insist that they are "good," that they just care about ecology and saving the planet from pollution and wars, etc. But the truth is, witchcraft is witchcraft, and it is all demonic whether it is imagined to be good or not. According to the Bible, communicating with any spirit other than the Spirit of God is the same as worshiping the devil. That includes visiting mediums to contact dead relatives, praying to Buddha or Krishna, consulting spirits of Eastern mysticism for health purposes, or trying to communicate with any other entity.

Setting people free from demons that entered through witchcraft can be difficult—not necessarily because these demons are stronger, but simply because the sacrifices, ceremonies, and rituals were done with the full consent of the victim. However, people involved in witchcraft can be set free from whatever curse or demon has entered their lives. No one is ever too far gone! The power of Jesus Christ and His sacrifice on the cross is far greater than Satan or any of his evil spirits.

Nicholas

Nicholas is another example from Johannesburg, South Africa. When we prayed for him in deliverance services, Nicholas would manifest evil spirits wildly, requiring four or five strong men to hold him down. While manifesting he had much more strength than a normal man his size, his body would be twisted and contorted into impossible shapes, and he would know personal things about people around him. If allowed, this demon would fight viciously until Nicholas was bleeding from a cut somewhere on his body. This particular demon wanted to see blood.

From interviews we discovered that everything began years before his birth; his father had sacrificed a bull to the spirits of his dead ancestors and asked for prosperity. His father did indeed become prosperous and had many businesses, houses, and cars, but from that time on the main demon considered the family his. Nicholas's older brother became mentally disturbed and had to be institutionalized—all because he refused to sacrifice to the spirits of his ancestors like his father regularly did. When Nicholas followed his brother's lead and wanted no part in his father's wealth because of its links to witchcraft, the demons brought suicidal thoughts, confusion, and sickness. But as he came to church he discovered how to fight this evil with the power of God, and he began to see victories for the first time in his life.

Consulting Mediums

The majority of black South Africans grow up being taught that the spirits of their dead ancestors can help them receive what they need from God. This is the common belief all over the African continent and in certain Asian countries as well. In fact, they fear that if they don't satisfy their ancestors with sacrifices and specific rituals that—just like Nicholas—they'll be sick, unemployed, or suffer from some terrible problem. It's not uncommon to see people walking around wearing a goat skin bracelet from a recent blood sacrifice to appease the ancestors, or to hear about them sacrificing chickens, goats, or bulls and possibly even drinking or washing in the blood of these animals. For all the sacrifices they make and all the attempts to appease the spirits, it doesn't take much to see that their ancestors haven't relieved them from the poverty, starvation, disease, and violence that have plagued Africa for centuries.

This extreme type of behavior may seem strange to someone in the Western world, but it is very normal for someone in Africa. Just as the Bible teaches, it is a big opening for the devil. By trusting in their ancestors as mediators, they reject Jesus as the unique and sole mediator between God and man, and they reject His precious sacrifice on the cross. As people reach out to the spiritual world for the help they need, the demons enter their lives to destroy them, and their victims have no hope as long as they do not know the truth about Jesus. This is just one more reason why missionaries and servants of God, who are willing to give their lives for the sake of the lost, are so needed in countries such as these. God the Father made His position on these things very clear when He said, "There shall not be found among you anyone who makes his son or his daughter pass through the fire, one who uses divination, one who practices witchcraft, or one who interprets omens, or a sorcerer, or one who casts a spell, or a medium, or a spiritist, or one who calls up the dead. For whoever does these things is detestable to the Lord" (Deuteronomy 18:10-12).

Here in the U.S. we have our own variety of questionable spiritual activities, which some people consider harmless and fun. To us they might seem much more civilized than ancestor worship in Africa, but spiritually speaking, they are just as dangerous—maybe even more so. There is a growing interest in contacting the dead or other spirits through mediums. TV has always had its share of psychics and mediums who claim to contact dead loved ones, giving demons the chance to pretend to be our relatives and tell us what we want to hear.

Maybe your dead Uncle Harry was there the night you broke your leg at the ice rink twenty years ago. When the medium recounts the story, it seems that old Uncle Harry is right there in the room. But evil spirits were also at the ice rink, and they are able to tell the story to the medium. In fact, there's a good chance that they were the ones who caused you to break your leg in the first place! The spirit of Uncle Harry, according to the Bible, can be either in paradise or Hades, and the entity that is speaking is really nothing more than a demonic spirit pretending to be your uncle—in the hope that you will let him guide you. That is why the Bible equates consulting mediums with worshiping the devil.

Astrology, Tarot Cards and Ouija Boards

Horoscopes, fortune-tellers, and tarot card readers are no different than mediums. Things that are used to discover what's going to happen before it happens are very tempting, but if God has not revealed it to you it's because He knows that you don't need to know. The Word of God speaks specifically about astrology and consulting the stars and how they fall into the ridiculous trap of worshiping the creation instead of the Creator (Deuteronomy 4:19). The stars have no intelligence or plan except what God has determined for them; they are simply a reflection of His glory and power. If we see order and beauty in them, we should go to the source of that beauty rather than wasting time reading messages into it.

As we've said before, evil spirits want us to believe in any spirit or power other than the Lord because, in that way, we would be worshiping them. The mystical powers that seem to work through Ouija boards and tarot cards are not a joke and should never be seen as a harmless slumber party game. If what is foretold through these things comes true, it is because demonic spirits are free to make them happen by the willingness of the people involved. Spirits do what they can to cause predictions to come true to convince us of their truth. Those people who think they are tapping into some "cosmic force" are consulting demons, who make people dependent on them and use predictions to destroy their lives and families. Once they have deceived their victims, they will come in to "occupy" the minds and hearts of those who believe in them because they are living in rebellion to the Word of God.

New Age Movement

The New Age movement, along with transcendental meditation, Eastern religions, martial arts, and yoga bring with them alternate philosophies of life. They teach that "all religions lead to God," "we are all gods," "you need to empty your mind," as well as a belief in reincarnation, gods and goddesses of nature, feng shui, crystals, and much more. These ideas are demonic because they seek power and guidance from spiritual forces other than the Lord Jesus. In this world there are only two spirits: the Spirit of God and the spirit of the devil. Evil spirits are nothing more than beings who execute the devil's will, and when someone tries to contact them, the spirits step right in to begin their job of killing, stealing, and destroying. Christ Jesus plainly said, "I am the way and the truth and the life. No one comes to the Father except by Me" (John 14:6).

Trauma and Abuse

Extreme fear, feelings of hopelessness, anger, guilt, and hatred are commonly what abuse and trauma leave in their wake. It's not uncommon for people to be crippled from these experiences many years after the actual abuse has ended. Some never recover, not because there is no hope, but because they never receive the spiritual help they need to be set free. Medical treatment and psychological counseling is helpful, but they can only deal with these wounds on a physical level. The real truth is that demonic forces work through the attacker to create much more than physical or emotional wounds; they damaged the spirit of the victim.

Too many women involved in an abusive relationship fear the pain and the rage they face at the hand of their husband or boyfriend, but they are trapped in a mindset that tells them they can't leave or that somehow they deserve the abuse. If children are involved, the results can be devastating, even if the kids are not themselves victims of the abuse. Sarah is a sad example of how demons of rage passed from her husband into her children. Her sons are only adolescents, but already they show signs of uncontrollable emotional swings and a lack of respect for their parents. They look on the weakness of their mother with frustration and disgust and the violence of their father with fear. When Sarah tried to leave her husband, at the urging of her family and friends, she made the first few steps to separate but then turned in anger against all those who were trying to help her and defiantly went back to the misery of her abusive marriage.

Demons feed on pain, suffering, and heartache, but the great power of the Lord Jesus erases all of that when evil spirits are cast out. Scars remain, but the painful and unbearable wounds are healed.

Unforgiveness

Unforgiveness is linked to grudges, selfishness, hatred, and other harmful attitudes, and it is one of the basic characteristics of Satan and his demons. Wherever there is unforgiveness, a person is in grave danger of becoming oppressed or possessed because he is rebelling against the direct command of the Lord Jesus. He is also blocking himself from receiving forgiveness from God, and without that he has no hope for eternity (see Matthew 6:14,15; 18:35; Mark 11:25,26; Luke 23:34).

Luiza

Luiza came to us in desperation because she felt like her life was cursed. Even though she was intelligent and well-schooled, she couldn't succeed in any job that she had. She felt that people were always against her, trying to block her from receiving the wages that were rightfully hers. But, digging deeper, we discovered that her worst problem was the horrible fear and anger she had carried with her for twenty years—ever since she witnessed her father and brother shot to death before her eyes. She still remembered every detail, even the people in the car who had chased her father down, laughing as he lay bleeding on the doorstep of her house.

As I prayed for her, Luiza quickly manifested demons who boasted about the deaths of many men in her family. They were at that moment causing a cancer in one of her brothers, and they were determined to steal his life as well. When I cast the demons out, Luiza felt free for the first time in years, but I explained that as long as she held unforgiveness in her heart against her father's murderers, those demons would easily return. I told her that her enemy was the devil, not the men who shot her family, and that she had to hate the devil, love her enemies, and forgive those who had hurt her. I challenged her to forgive her enemies that very day. In the twenty years since the murders, she had never been able to make that prayer. She had forgiven everyone else but could not even say the words when it came to the killers. Though it was incredibly hard, she began to repeat a prayer after me, but she started to stutter badly, unable to continue. After challenging her to go ahead and do it by faith, she finally said the words. Then, again and again, louder and louder, she forgave the men who had killed her father and brother.

It was a very emotional experience for everyone present, but it was more than simple feelings; it was spiritual determination on the part of Luiza to obey God's commands. I knew that it might take time for her to truly feel that she had forgiven them and to feel a true desire for them to be saved, but the important thing was that she had begun the process.

True forgiveness is impossible for us to do by our own strength, which is why it is such a powerful weapon against the devil. Satan wants us to equate forgiveness with weakness, but forgiveness is one of the most powerful attitudes in life—and we have a holy, perfect example of it in our Lord Jesus on the cross.

Addictions

Many addictions that are common today are not mentioned in the Bible because drugs and other substances had not yet been discovered. Yet the principle of addiction is condemned. When a person's consciousness is altered by alcohol or drugs to the extent that they no longer have self-control and their flesh is allowed to take over, they are willfully allowing demonic forces to enter their thoughts and dwell inside of them; before they realize it, they are driven and controlled by their addictions (see Matthew 16:24-27).

Cigarettes and other forms of tobacco are seen as acceptable "vices," but they are life-threatening addictions that can cause cancer, heart disease, and emphysema and can harm the lives of children and others who inhale the second-hand smoke. Addiction to gambling goes against the principle that hard work is rewarded; it's driven by greed and the demonic desire to get something for nothing—even though that is the exact opposite of what actually happens. Addictions can vary from pornography to prescription drugs. They create an obsessive state of mind that believes satisfaction and happiness can be found outside the Word of God, ignoring the fact that "Man shall not live on bread alone, but on every word that proceeds out of the mouth of God" (Matthew 4:4).

Sexual Immorality

No one wants to be told how to live their lives, especially when it comes to their sexual behavior. Homosexuality is explicitly condemned in the Bible (see Romans 1:26,27; Genesis 19:4,5), as are other perversions of the beautiful and intimate physical relationship intended for a husband and wife (see 1 Corinthians 6:18; Galatians 5:19-21). When a husband has sexual relations with another woman, the attitude of unfaithfulness that he has toward his wife cannot help but affect his relationship with God. Can a man be faithful to God while he is being unfaithful to his wife? Never.

Unfaithfulness is more than just a weakness in character, and, as mentioned in Chapter 3, there is a spiritual dimension in the sexual relationship that binds a couple to one another in a holy and mysterious way, making them one flesh (see Ephesians 5:32). Treating something so holy and pure in a selfish way, with no lasting commitment of love, defiles the lives of both people involved. The apostle Paul teaches that our bodies are the temple of the Holy Spirit, and with this type of sin we are defiling that temple (see 1 Corinthians 6:18-20). This is exactly the kind of activity that the devil loves—to take what is holy and make it impure and filthy—and in this way he easily enters people's lives.

Fear

We don't normally consider fear to be a sin, much less something on a par with drug addiction, but it is just as much an opening for demonic forces to enter our lives. Fear is a clear sign that we are not trusting in God and that the lies of the devil are at work in our hearts (see Romans 8:15; Hebrews 2:15; 1 John 4:18). Fear paralyzes us emotionally, but it has physical manifestations, too. Ulcers, weakened immune systems, cancer, and many other conditions can be seen in people who have the demon of fear at work in their lives. Fear feeds the disease, which creates more pain, which in turn generates more fear. Fearful people drive others away from them; even family members who love them find their presence a burden because of their constant complaints and paranoia.

A person who is truly converted and has Jesus in his heart is filled with the peace that transcends all understanding, even when problems and threats are swirling around him (see Philippians 4:6,7). Fear attacks us all from time to time, but those who have faith deal with it quickly, holding on to the Word of God until His peace takes over. But a person who constantly lives in a state of fear, seeing problems where there are none, is a person who is demonized.

Love of Money, Power, and Position

It's a given that most people want to be in a better position than they presently are, but obsession can lead people to perform the most evil acts in order to get what they want. Through this desire, violent gangs arise, racial supremist groups act out their hate crimes, and cold-blooded political regimes come into power. Love of power can drive wealthy and successful businessmen to destroy the lives of their own families in a frantic search to exalt themselves. Wars of genocide, the slaughter of innocent people all over the world, began with this open door to demonic activity. It can begin in the heart of one insignificant person, but it has the capacity to fester and grow until it manifests its destruction on entire nations.

This demon is so prevalent in Western society that we often take it for granted, as it cloaks itself in the driving energy of capitalism. Some even praise this desire for success as part of the "American dream." But the lust for power at any cost is nothing more than a carbon copy of the desires of Lucifer himself when he craved the position of the Most High. This spirit of greed can inhabit anyone—from the gang-banger on the street to the most impressive and influential leaders on the planet—but no matter how strong they may appear, they are lost and will be destroyed by their own actions.

Pride

Few people would ever admit that they were proud, and most consider pride to be the same as arrogance. But pride is something more than just being stuck-up or egotistical. It can be a subtle and deceptive characteristic that hides itself under the guise of meekness or timidity. It is nothing more than a stubborn refusal to be obedient to God and a desire to live according to one's own ideas. Pride can be loud and boastful or cold and defiant. No matter how pride reveals itself, it is evil and destructive.

Laura is a quiet and shy teenager who comes regularly to church with her mother and enjoys having fun with the other kids. But Laura's shyness is a cover for a very proud and stubborn character. When she is caught in the act of doing what is wrong, she refuses to apologize and gives a long list of reasons why she just had to do what she did. Words of discipline and correction are first met with light jokes but later with a stone-faced refusal to repent for her wrong. Appealing to her sense of kindness toward those she has hurt has no effect. Even the fear of opening her life to demons is met with a shrug—though she has seen many demons manifest before, even in her own mother.

Laura's apparent sweetness is just a façade for a demonic presence inside her. The fruit of her life shows a love of this world and a hatred for the things of God—even though she was baptized in

water and comes regularly to church. Pride is often associated with
the rich or famous, but it can work in the hearts of even the poorest beggar who refuses to admit he needs to change his way of life.
Pride was what blinded the Pharisees and Sadducees into rejecting
their long-awaited Messiah—and what caused Jesus to call them
"sons of hell."

It shouldn't be a surprise to know that pride is alive and well
among the religious people of today, inflating the egos of pastors,
evangelists, ministry leaders, and their followers. When a pastor
talks more about how people were blessed because of his ministry
rather than by the Lord Jesus, you know he has that same spirit. If a
pastor's wife feels threatened by church members who are more
knowledgeable or talented than herself, she could turn the church
into a miserable place of tensions, jealousy, and back-biting because
she is not free from that demon of pride. Pride is what turned
Lucifer into Satan, and its power to blind us to the truth cannot be
underestimated. "The Lord detests all the proud of heart. Be sure of
this: They will not go unpunished" (Proverbs 16:5).

Rebellion

Rebellion against those whom God has placed in authority over
us goes hand in hand with the love of power and position. It is the
action that Lucifer took to rise up against God in heaven and what
determined his banishment for eternity. The rebellious teenager has
been accepted as a normal rite of passage for the average family; we
accept it and hope that in time they will learn to settle down and get
along with their parents. But rebellion is more than actions. It is an
attitude of the heart that has spiritual ramifications. When a child
rebels against his parents, he is rebelling against God, the final
authority over his parents. In the same way, a wife who rebels
against her husband, a man who rebels against his boss, a church
member who rebels against the leadership of his church, and a citi-
zen who rebels against the laws of his government are all showing
hostility toward God. Rebellion against God reveals an alliance with
the devil.

True, these leaders set in place on this earth are sinful people
who make mistakes, but God understands our weaknesses and has

provided His Spirit to give us wisdom to work in submission even when our leaders fail. Of course, if our leaders try to force us to sin, we have to obey God first. In such a situation, disobedience to these authorities is correct. Christians in a Muslim country who continue to pray to Jesus and read their illegal Bibles are pleasing God while at the same time breaking the law. But in situations where no sin is involved, an attitude of submission toward those placed over us is a way to protect ourselves from the attacks of the devil and allows God to bless us—even when our authorities are not kind or understanding of our needs. "For rebellion is like the sin of divination, and arrogance like the evil of idolatry" (1Samuel 15:23).

Time to Fight Back

With modern science and psychology offering an explanation for every phobia, syndrome, and tendency, we have to be careful not to take their word over the Word of God. There is an invisible spiritual struggle all around us, whether or not we believe it or like it. If we don't take the initiative and attack these demonic forces with faith in the name of Jesus, we'll become their next victims. By succeeding in their attacks against us, they may succeed in finding a way to force themselves into our families. It's either win or lose.

The categories listed here are just the beginning of the many ways the devil can try to enter our lives. The devil is not lazy. If we allow him an entrance, he'll find it and force his way in. Even when he does not come into our hearts to possess us, he still works outside of us, trying to find a way to oppress us in some way. If the devil is so aggressive and unrelenting, shouldn't we who have given our lives to Jesus be even more aggressive and unrelenting against his schemes? Some Christians seem to think not, but the Bible shows us that we must be armed and ready, not only to defend ourselves but to fight back.

"Be of sober spirit, be on the alert. Your adversary, the devil, prowls around like a roaring lion, seeking someone to devour" (1 Peter 5:8).

CHAPTER FIVE

Spirits of Division

Demons work to destroy our lives in such subtle ways that we ignorantly blame people around us—our bosses, our families, the government, or society in general—for problems that are nothing more than demonic. Everyone wants to find a way out of their problems, and many are willing to fight long and hard to overcome them. But if we don't know who is responsible for these problems, we end up swinging punches at the air, attacking others unfairly, developing hatreds and grudges, and getting ourselves into worse difficulties than before. This is a big joke for the devil. When we get entangled in lawsuits that drain our money or become overwhelmed with fear or anger to the point that our bodies develop pains and diseases, we feed the devil's ravenous appetite to see more suffering.

Forgiveness, peace, harmony, love for our enemies, solid families, caring churches—these, according to the Bible, are all important foundations for our lives as Christians. But they are so hard to do! Living a life that is right before God requires the supernatural power of the Holy Spirit enabling us to do things that go against our natural desires. Without this power, we could make a good attempt to live in love and understanding, but our sinful nature makes us incapable of doing all that we need to do. And not knowing that the terrible actions of people around us can be changed by our prayers and faith can cause us to react to them in ungodly ways. We've all heard the expression, "Love the sinner, hate the sin," but it should go even further and say, "Love the sinner, hate the sin, and drive out the demon that is behind it all so that it never happens again!"

Divisive Spirits Are Prevalent

"I make everybody hate her!" the demon shouted as it manifested in the young woman for whom I was praying. "I make her children stubborn so that she'll ignore them!"

This is what I call the demon of division. It works in families, in marriages, between brother and sister, mother and child. It drives people away from its victim, and it creates negative feelings in others so that the victim will never get hired for a job or chosen to receive any kindness. This woman was on welfare, unmarried, and in such a deep depression that she barely had enough energy to feed and clothe her children each day. The various fathers of her children had all wanted to marry her, but one by one they gave up as she found ways to anger them and push them out of her life.

When I asked her if she knew what had happened after we set her free, she was surprised to know that she had been demon possessed. She knew her life had been miserable, but she had always tried to be a "good Christian," according to her own standards. As I counseled her more after the service, she told me she had often heard voices telling her that she couldn't trust anyone and that she would always be a big failure. When people would try to get close to her and show her love, she would feel afraid and do something negative to drive them away. Yet deep inside she was so lonely and longed for the closeness of a happy family or a good friend. As weeks went by, she began to make sense of her irrational behavior. She realized that what she thought were her own desires were actually demonic forces manipulating her to live a life of suffering.

Demons are quite deft at manipulating the thoughts and emotions of people they enter. Demons of division, along with other sorts of evil spirits, are working around the clock to destroy lives, but they are rarely identified and cast out. In Chapter 3 we discussed various signs of possession, listing the main ways that demons work in people's lives. We can add divisive spirits to that list and devote an entire chapter to their discussion because they are so prevalent and little recognized in our society.

When demons work in and around us, they can be so subtle that no one recognizes they are there. Only those with spiritual discernment can spot their work. How many kids do we see who are loners, ostracized by their peers and frightened by the rejection they face day after day? How many parents are frustrated to the point of rage when their children refuse to respond to their instructions, their love, or their discipline? How many people are alone and unable to find a spouse, even when they seem to have a decent personality and appearance? Demons work in a person's mind, affecting attitudes, determining who is looked upon with favor and who is looked upon with disdain. Yes, demons do have that power—as long as the presence of God is not there to protect us.

"A poor man is shunned by all his relatives—how much more do his friends avoid him! Though he pursues them with pleading, they are nowhere to be found" (Proverbs 19:7). The poor man in this verse is not just a guy with no money. This man is spiritually poor, one who lacks the richness of God's power and protection that comes from a deep, trusting relationship with Him. There are many examples in the Bible of how the Spirit of God touched the hearts of people to create feelings of either approval or disapproval toward others, depending on the situation. In a similar way, the devil infiltrated the thoughts and feelings of people in the Bible to make them hate those who were innocent or love those who were evil.

Joseph, Daniel, Esther, and Others...

Joseph was hated by his brothers because his father loved him the best, and their hatred led them almost to the point of murder. But the faith that Joseph had in God, and in the dreams that God had given him, caused even his captors to look upon him with kindness and trust—and eventually he reached the second highest position in the country of Egypt. Because Joseph was living according to God's ways and had God's character, he was able to love and forgive his brothers who had treated him so badly. The Spirit he had within him drew him close to all who were around him. It caused others to love him and caused him to love others no matter how difficult the circumstances.

Daniel was a young man who found favor in the eyes of the evil kings of Babylon, though the royal advisors were filled with jealousy. **Esther** was a simple Jewish girl who was chosen to become the queen above all the beautiful girls of Persia. By her dedication to God and His chosen people, Esther was able to overturn the decree of her unbelieving husband, King Xerxes to annihilate the Jews. **The woman of noble character,** of whom King Solomon speaks in the book of Proverbs, brings honor to her husband, and because of her life of faith in God, he is respected by the elders of the land. Young **Jesus** grew "in wisdom and stature, and in favor with God and man" (Luke 2:52).

The Bible also gives examples of those who suffered rejection, loss, and loneliness at the hands of the devil. **Lot,** the nephew of Abraham, was humiliated and threatened by unbelievers; he lost his home and his wife after choosing to live in the evil city of Sodom. **Eli** the priest had rebellious and selfish sons who treated the things of God in an unholy way. Though Eli loved God, he and his family were cursed by God because Eli did not raise his sons in a godly way. Although **King Saul** had been anointed by God, through the prophet Samuel, to be the first king of Israel, Saul lost God's blessing when he decided to live according to his own ideas and make excuses to God. His own people turned their hearts away from him and instead toward the young shepherd boy, David, who had killed the giant by his courage and faith. When God allowed Satan to attack **Job,** his family was destroyed and his wife and friends became more of a curse than a blessing to him. But when God rewarded him after he proved faithful, Job was doubly blessed: God returned all that the devil had stolen away, and Job was held in honor by all around him. These are just a few examples of how the devil's work in a person's life drives a wedge of separation between them and those around them.

Manipulating Minds

In Africa an odd manifestation of this sort of demon attacked people in the form of what they called "pig lice." Small insects would roam around the person's body, especially on their head and eyebrows, biting them and causing them to itch and feel pain. When Jeffrey told me about his problems with pig lice, he explained that they would only appear in important situations, like during job interviews or when visiting elders in his family who could help him out financially. His wife said she had seen the lice crawling all over him and that they would disappear as soon as his interviews or special meetings would end. When they appeared, he would twitch and swat at his face, lose all concentration, and say the wrong things. He was unemployed for many years, although he had an education that under normal circumstances would get him a decent job. They tried all sorts of doctors and herbalists, but they didn't realize that there were no such insects; demonic spirits were the cause of it all. Among all the pastors I worked with in Africa, we have prayed for tens of thousands of people who were attacked with this affliction—and not one of us has ever actually seen these "pig lice." Those who are demonized may see these things on themselves or on other people, but those who are free do not.

I have never heard of anyone in the U.S. with this particular demonic attack, but I have met many who suffer the demons of division, which basically have the same destructive effect on the people around them. A demon works in the life of a person to defile them through sin and to see them suffer and live in misery—to make them lose all hope that God is real and will save them from their problems. As a person with the demon of division walks into a room full of people, the demon begins its work to twist the thoughts of those who are unspiritual and cause them to feel a subtle dislike toward the person who is demonized. These demons are able to work freely in the minds of those who are already possessed or oppressed by other evil spirits; the demons join forces to cause more dislike, jealously, hatred, gossip, and hurt feelings. The victim may never realize that the problem is a spiritual one coming from within himself, and instead he blames the insensitivity of everyone around him. He is driven to become untrusting, reclusive, resentful, angry, and mean-spirited to hide behind the fear of more rejection. As a result, demons have an even greater opportunity to work in that person's life through his fear, unforgiveness, and sense of despair that no one wants to help him. The hurt feelings he suffers are from others who have been affected by their own demons, and they fight a losing battle when they try to confront people rather than their true enemy.

So many self-help books have been written about boosting our self-esteem and how we need to love ourselves. I believe this is the world's attempt to combat this demonic force of greed, jealously, and stepping on each other to get to the top that works so much in our Western society. But when it comes down to practical, day-to-day living, telling ourselves that we are special people and deserve to be treated nicely is not going to remove the demonic spirit of division that utterly destroys families and relationships.

The hardest part of setting people free from this demon is convincing them to stop blaming everyone else for their problems and to gear their anger toward the devil. The desire for vengeance is so strong in people who have suffered a great deal of injustice in their lives that they feel it's unrealistic to simply forgive and ignore what people have done in the past. Trusting in God's judgment and God's vengeance, as Romans 12 teaches us, requires a great deal of humility and submission to God, but that is the beginning of the process of complete freedom for those in this situation.

Recognizing the Spirit of Division

Even before people learn how to forgive and put their problems in the proper perspective, God is ready to begin setting them free from these spirits of division, but first they must be open to receive prayer and to learn how to fight in a spiritual way. Evelyn counseled and prayed for a woman named Sandra, whose husband was regularly involved in substance abuse and ridiculed her for her newfound faith in God. Sandra felt so belittled by him that she began to live as a stranger in her own house. Though she understood that he had demons, she would unwisely tell him to his face that he was full of the devil, which would send him into a rage. Her faith had taken her out of drugs and alcohol herself, but she didn't yet know how to bring healing to her marriage. As Evelyn and I spent time explaining how to fight against the root of the problem—by prayer rather than by physical confrontation—we began to see changes both in Sandra and in her husband.

Showing love to those who are difficult to love is more than just obeying Christ's command to love our enemies; it is an incredible weapon that destroys hidden demons causing anger and division. With each act of love and kindness toward her husband, even when those actions were rejected, Sandra persisted in the faith that her actions were a pleasing sacrifice to the Lord Jesus. Through faith and action she knew she would defeat the power of the enemy that wanted to break up her marriage.

It took a week before she saw a change in her husband. He began to stay home more often and turn away invitations from his friends to go out drinking. He surprised her with breakfast in bed one morning, and he sent her off to church to make sure she prayed for him. He began to play with their children instead of shouting at them, and finally, after many months of prayer, he has given up drugs and alcohol and has given his life to Jesus because of the faithful testimony of Sandra's love.

Our fight against the devil begins with prayers: rebuking, commanding, and casting spirits out, tying them up, burning them, putting them under our feet, and demanding that they leave our lives. But the fight doesn't end there. Each prayer offered in faith is powerful and effective, but the actions and attitudes of our lives continue the fight into everyday life. Sandra learned that godly love is a weapon to destroy the strongholds of the devil, and those demons of division and addictions were under constant siege by her attitudes of faith. Jeffrey, the man afflicted with "pig lice," no longer felt the attack after receiving prayers in the church, but he was afraid to go to any job interview, anticipating their return. But when he took on an attitude of faith, and felt a holy anger against the devil for what he had stolen from his life, Jeffrey went to find a job, determined that he was free. Now he is a very successful bank manager and has a beautiful family—a complete change from his former way of life.

There are many more examples. Parents with rebellious children who learn to fight the evil spirits that are driving their family apart and find a new love binding them all together. Victims who have been treated unjustly in court cases are able to see God's justice at work when they pray with faith and tie up the demons of division. People who were owed money reach the hearts of those who were blocking their finances and receive what was justly due.

Demons work in subtle ways, and we often are deceived into thinking that solutions to the problems demons cause are found in lawyers, doctors, employers, therapists, and so on. People waste so much time agonizing over the details of who did what and who said what, when the demons inside are orchestrating the whole miserable situation. In the seventies, a popular Christian saying was "Jesus is the answer." Few people have ever realized the depth of that statement. For many people, Jesus is the answer to finding eternal salvation, happiness, peace, a new moral code, and a church family, but they find that the other grueling details of life are just as difficult and painful as before.

Jesus died on the cross for us to bring us into God's presence. The veil of separation that hung in the Temple was torn in two from top to bottom when He died, signifying that we can boldly go into His presence and be blessed as His children, even though we are terrible sinners. The blood He shed for us destroyed all the power of the devil, all our sicknesses, all our sins—the punishment for all the evil in this world was paid for by His precious sacrifice. Because of that, we can find freedom from all the attacks of the devil, no matter how strong or terrible they are. But just the fact that Jesus paid the price is not enough for us to see our victory; we have to fight in His name and with His authority to destroy those demons. God has already given us every weapon we need, and, through the example of His Son and through His Word, He has taught us how to counterattack the work of the enemy. Our victory is guaranteed—as long as we remain in Him and follow in His footsteps.

The demons of division are weak and powerless in the light of our Lord and Savior. When we come against them in prayer, cast them out of our lives, learn to fight against them by our daily attitudes of faith, love, and stubborn perseverance, they have no choice but to run away from us in fear. Families can be reunited, success can replace failure, love can replace hatred, and forgiveness can replace anger.

CHAPTER SIX

Spirits of Doubt:
the Spiritual Cancer

Alan was coming to church on a regular basis, praying, fighting in his faith, and trying his best to overcome demons of addiction, depression, and violence that had been working in his life for more than twenty years. He believed in God and in His power to set people free, but when it came to his healing, his thoughts were clouded by overwhelming doubts and skepticism. Every morning he would wake up with an oppressive heaviness hanging over him with vivid thoughts that God would never, ever set him free. His mind would race through a myriad different arguments on why I, as his pastor, had to be a fraud, how the Bible just couldn't apply to him, how nothing had changed at all despite months of prayers, and how he should just give up and and go back to his old life. He would at times appear in the church, so low, so negative, even challenging me to prove that he was wrong. Praise God he would come for help, because if left in that state of mind, he could have gone and immersed himself in the addictions and violence of the past to "escape" the torment in his mind.

Alan had a serious struggle with the demons of doubt, something that all of us have struggled with from time to time. The difference with Alan is that it was demonic possession that blinded him from the truth he wanted to believe and pushed him to make decisions over and over again that he would bitterly regret. These demons of doubt work hardest among those who know the Word of God, who know they have to change their lives, and who want to live victoriously for Christ. Without doubts, these people (who make up the majority of Christians in America) would be overcoming the devil at every turn. The devil has no power to steal away our salvation or our faith. But what he can do is to nullify our faith and render it powerless—through doubts.

James says that he who doubts should not think he will receive anything from God: "But he must ask in faith without any doubting, for the one who doubts is like the surf of the sea, driven and tossed by the wind. For that man ought not to expect that he will receive anything from the Lord, being a double-minded man, unstable in all his ways" (James 1:6). But Jesus said that if we have even the tiniest faith of a mustard seed, we can move mountains and that "…nothing will be impossible to you" (Matthew 17:20). In other words, with faith we can get the impossible, with doubts we'll never get anything! It simple and straightforward—but it's so hard for many people to get a handle on.

For some, doubts are just a normal part of their way of life. Some even consider doubt a sign of intelligence; people think that they're protecting themselves by being cautious about what they believe and accept into their hearts. Yes, God want us to be cautious and have discernment, but if we allow caution to override the mighty promises of the Word of God, we've passed the point of godly discernment and fallen into the unbelief of the devil.

Doubts Seem Rational

Alan's doubts appeared to be so rational as they bombarded his mind. It seemed to make sense that the prayers weren't working because he was feeling rotten. The demon of doubt disguised itself as Alan's own mind, taking over whenever Alan fell for the trap of analyzing the things going on around him. But every time we would speak and pray together, casting out the demons at work in his life, he would feel an enormous change come over him—a lightness, as if someone had lifted a heavy weight from his shoulders. He would look at me and say, "How do you do that? I can't believe I feel so good! I didn't think it would work this time. How couldn't I see that God has been blessing me over the last few days? It's so clear now!"

Alan had been thinking negative things, and yet at the same time, it wasn't just Alan. There were demonic forces behind his thoughts, destroying his faith to overcome. Even though he was conscious and aware of what was going on, he could also tell that something was wrong—that he wasn't thinking the thoughts that he wanted to think. Then there came other arguments: "How do I know these attacks are a demon and not just my own sinful nature? Why doesn't God just take away the tempatations and lusts? How will I ever know what is a demon and what is just me?" And with all these thoughts, the doubts kept coming back to destroy his life.

At almost every service he attended, Alan would stay behind to receive extra prayer, and many of those times he would manifest demons that were at turns violent, babbling, and argumentative. "You're wasting your time. Nothing's happening. This is me Alan— I'm not a demon. You can pray all day long, nothing's gonna change. You're not strong enough. You don't have enough faith." The babbling demonic voice droned on and on saying the same, calm, rational sounding garbage whenever it was not trying to choke me or throw me to the floor. I ignored it and kept on praying, rebuking the demons of doubt, the demons of addiction, and the generational spirits that had been working in the men of his family for more than five generations. As I prayed, the voice kept trying to make excuses why I couldn't cast it out, that it wasn't a demon at all. But when the demons would finally be cast out, Alan would open his eyes and begin to cry with relief, knowing that the oppressive thoughts and lusts were gone. As weeks and months went by, he finally realized that all those old thoughts were not his thoughts at all, just the confusion of evil spirits. They had disguised themselves as his own intellect, but they were, in fact, demons of doubt entering to contaminate his faith so that his prayers would be absolutely powerless. (For Alan's complete testimony in his own words, see the Postscript.)

Some people, like Alan, are possessed with the spirit of doubt and need it to be cast out of their lives. Others are just tormented with this demon and can resist it by refusing to listen and by rebuking its lies. Everyone on the face of the earth has been attacked with doubts when it comes to faith in God. It's one of the most common and deceptive demons around, and through it millions of lives have been and are being destroyed.

The Great Immobilizer

Doubt is the great immobilizer of lives. It brings progress to a screeching halt. The terrorist attacks on September 11 are just one example of that. Out of the thousands of flights in operation that day, four ended in tragedy; as a result, the entire airline industry was paralyzed and close to collapsing for months afterwards. Doubts in people's minds questioned whether airplanes would ever be reliable again, and these doubts were enough to bring some of these companies to the brink of bankruptcy. The stock market plunged, tourist resorts were abandoned, even shopping malls were left empty as the majority of Americans barricaded themselves in their homes—all because of doubt.

Just as faith gives birth to boldness, strength, and joy, doubt spawns fear, weakness, and depression—just like a cancer branches out and spreads from one organ to another. I remember praying for an old grandmother in Africa who was dying of breast cancer. Her tumor was so far gone that she smelled of rotting flesh. It was hard to even be close to her, but she persisted in asking for prayer. In December of 1993, she told me that the doctors wouldn't see her anymore; they recommended that her family prepare her funeral because she had less than two weeks to live. But she was defiant and determined. She never cried or complained, although she was in great pain, and she kept coming to the church despite her difficulty in walking.

I traveled to start a church in another city during that time, and I have to admit I forgot all about her. A year later I returned and was amazed to see a woman run up to me with a big smile on her face.

I recognized her instantly. She showed me a small scar on her chest where her tumor once was and said, "I'm healed! I'm really healed. The doctor says that all my cancer is gone with no operation—only Jesus!"

This woman had every reason to doubt God. Her incredible pain, her growing tumor, her smell of death, the discouragement of her doctors, and the tears of her family were all valid reasons for her to believe in death. But she was so determined to see a miracle that she believed despite all the doubts and "logic" of the devil, and, weak as she was, she bulldozed her way through the negative thoughts and found her complete healing!

I know of plenty of other people, however, who are in suffering and live in a world of doubts. They pray for healing or freedom, then lash out in anger at God for not answering their prayers. When I challenge them to reject the doubts, to hold on to Jesus and persevere in their faith, I run the risk of appearing insensitive and cruel, implying that they haven't done all that they can do. But what else can I say if that is what Jesus commands us to do? We can only receive a miracle by faith, and we can never expect an answer from God with doubts. The fight to destroy doubts can be a long and tedious one or a quick one—it all depends on the determination of the one searching for a miracle. Part of the fight comes from our prayers, rebuking the demons of doubt, but the most important part comes from refusing to listen to the devil's lies and determining that God's Word will come true.

The Bible says that the devil constantly accuses us, reminding us of our unworthiness and our sins. Because he knows that sin is what separates us from God, he infiltrates our thoughts with condemnation upon condemnation. He reminds us that we are sinners and that we have failed miserably to live a life that is right before God, but then he twists the Word of God and tells us that Jesus' death on the cross is not enough for us to be forgiven and made worthy to enter into God's presence. Each time we sin, the devil has us defeated. We are too ashamed to raise our eyes to heaven, and because of our shame, we feel convinced that we have no authority to fight against the devil anymore. Through those insidious doubts we become pathetic and defeated Christians.

Living by Faith

The Bible says, "But the righteous man shall live by faith" (Romans 1:17) Our righteousness is what gives us the ability to live by faith. When we are free from living in sin—not our daily sins, which we fall into and quickly repent of, but the sins that we willfully commit because of our desires—and we live in an attitude of humility and dependence on our Lord, we can easily reject doubts and live by faith. Righteousness is when we strive to live a sinless life in the understanding that we are sinful people and need constant forgiveness and mercy. Our faith that God has forgiven us and that he has raised us up to be His children makes us righteous before Him. Our righteousness depends more on our determination to live by faith than on being perfect. If God were only to bless us when we are perfect, we would all be heading for hell right now!

Faith allows us to understand that our God is loving, compassionate, kind, and eager to bless us even when we have completely messed up our lives. He is a tender, loving Father who is ready to erase our sins and cast them as far as the East is from the West. Yet doubts cause us to look at God as an angry judge, condemning, cold, and distant, who pounds His gavel and orders us to come back only after we've gotten our act together. I don't know how many times I've felt like this when I've prayed, almost feeling like prayer was useless because I had been so rotten. I knew I didn't deserve to have my prayers answered. I used to rationalize that the drug dealers on the corner could be heard by God because they didn't know better, but God expected more of me and I had failed Him and therefore I could never receive an answer to my prayers. Only as I developed a closer relationship to God did I understand how desperately I needed to run to Him after my failures, to seek His forgiveness and comfort, and to be set free from all the doubts that were paralyzing my faith.

Fear, Anxiety, and Worry Begin as Seeds of Doubt

After Adam and Eve sinned in the Garden of Eden, the serpent didn't even need to say a word; they were immediately ashamed and afraid of their closest, most loving friend, God. Their doubts as to whether God still loved them caused them to hide from Him and to invent excuses for why they had disobeyed Him. Sin broke their communion, and from then on they had to suffer the consequences. They had to fight against the spirit of doubt and all other demons that they had let loose on this earth through that one act.

Doubt is the mother of fear, anxiety, and worry. Through doubt, all sorts of demons can enter our lives to destroy us spiritually, emotionally, and physically. Doubt blocks us from reaching out to God and gives us what appears to be a rationale for accepting our problems. We get a false sense of security when we hold on to doubts: We feel that faith is too radical, and we don't want to stick out our necks to believe because then we might get hurt. Doubting seems safe and we think we are being cautious, but in the end it carries us further and further from God, our only hope.

Evelyn was afraid of even trying to have faith to be healed. What if she prayed and nothing happened? What if she tried to believe and God let her down? She was afraid to take that risk, and as a result, that attitude of doubt just grew and grew. Finally she learned how to reject it by seeing the miracles in others' lives.

If doubt is one of the greatest tools of the devil, then proving that God's power and goodness are for today is absolutely essential for the church. In a world that is being saturated in doubts more and more as time goes by, we need miracles, deliverance, healings, and transformations in people's lives. As we who believe attack the spirit of doubt, the glory of God will be revealed, faith will increase all around us, and the name of Jesus will be honored.

"I do believe; help my unbelief!" (Mark 9:24).

CHAPTER SEVEN

Constant Headaches

Seansay loved her parents. She loved the vacations, outings, and fun times that made up her favorite memories of the past. But she hated her father's alcoholism. The humiliating times that he would turn violent and cause a scene in public were memories she wished she could erase from her mind. Seansay and her mother lived in constant fear of what would happen next. When her father would calm down and stop drinking for a few months at a time, they would cross their fingers and hope that it would last forever. But, of course, the demons of addiction that wanted to control his life would always come back in full force to bring more arguments and misery to their household. From the time that Seansay was a little girl, she feared that her father might kill her mother in one of his drunken rages, yet she was too ashamed to speak freely about her fears to anyone else.

Seansay hated alcohol and addictions of any kind because of the horrible experiences she had gone through, and she was determined to live a completely different life as an adult, to have a stable life and career. When we met Seansay, she appeared strong, healthy, and in control of her life, but after hearing her story, we could see that her appearance was a cover for the misery she felt inside.

Though she refused to live the same life of addiction as her father, she began to suffer in other debilitating ways. Since high school she had experienced intense migraine headaches four or five times a week. She would force herself to work, trying her best to control her pain, but at times she wouldn't even be able to get out of bed. As the years passed and she tried to cope with the migraines by taking massive doses of painkillers, she developed a huge cancerous tumor on her ovary that grew so rapidly it almost took her life. After emergency surgery to remove all the surrounding organs, she was left with even more pain. She lost her job and, with all her medical bills piling up, had to declare bankruptcy.

Seansay was young and beautiful, but she felt old and cast aside by the world. She couldn't work, and her migraines were more unbearable than before. Even a trip to the post office became a huge ordeal that would exhaust her for days. She had insomnia and nightmares on a regular basis, and she felt like her body would never be able to heal. Seansay had resigned herself to enduring a life of suffering. But after hearing testimonies of healings from our church, a glimmer of hope caused her to come and try to use her faith. She came to us for prayer, and after a few weeks of learning about God's power and the reality of demons, Seansay was determined to cast out whatever it was in her life that was causing all this pain.

I prayed for her, and the chief demon that had been hiding in her mind and body manifested in a manner very much unlike Seansay. It was rude and defiant, and it even appeared drunk, laughing in a mocking way just like Seansay remembered her father doing in some of his most frightening rages. It was, strangely, the same demon that had caused addictions in her father. He spoke angrily that he had been in Seansay's life from the time she was born, entering her life through both her father and mother, but that he was unable to get Seansay to take drugs or alcohol as he wanted, because she so stubbornly refused to live that kind of life. So, as revenge for her stubbornness, he caused terrible headaches, accidents, financial losses, and medically unexplainable aches all over her body. When the demons were cast out, all the pain in her body left, and her migraines and insomnia stopped.

Seansay needed more than just one prayer of deliverance; she had to go through the process of giving her life more and more to the Lord and developing a real relationship with Him to strengthen her faith. But as she allowed God to transform her heart and life, the demons of the past were unable to return. Her health and energy is now restored, and, most importantly, she knows how to fight and overcome any problem that comes her way.

Seansay's example is an interesting one because her problems seemed to have nothing to do with addictions. She was never a substance abuser; rather, her most unbearable problems were the headaches. I have come to learn, from my own experience and the testimony of other pastors, that constant headaches require more than just painkillers: There is a spiritual battle going on in the lives of those who suffer this kind of physical problem.

When Headaches Are Demonic

Headaches are a normal part of our lives from time to time—when we don't get enough rest or proper nourishment, or when we've been straining our eyes at the computer or behind the wheel on a sunny day. There are all kinds of reasons for that slight throbbing feeling, and normally with an aspirin or two and a good night's sleep, we bounce right back. But there are kinds of headaches that just don't leave, no matter what you do. They become an unwelcome companion that after time is accepted as a part of life, even though they are unbearable. Painkillers, massages, and special diets can all help to a point, but the headaches seem to have a life and mind of their own, and just keep on attacking. This is clearly demonic.

Demons that create these kind of headaches are in a struggle of wills. The first evil spirit to enter a person automatically becomes the head (the "strong man" as Jesus call them in Matthew 12:29), and others that follow submit to him—unless other strong demons are invited, in which case a power struggle might ensue. For example, perhaps a person was born with a generational spirit that took control of his life, considering itself to be the chief demon of that person. If that person becomes involved in some demonic activity—the occult, witchcraft, addictions, false religions, etc.—he is inviting other strong demons into his life, and one of them may be unwilling to submit to the head demon.

In effect, the chief demon that feels he owns the person has a battle for position with the "new" demon that just arrived. Because neither wants to allow the other to become the chief, a conflict between the two dominant spirits results in constant, unbearable headaches. Though the Bible never speaks about this kind of power struggle among demons, it is something I have seen over and over again among those who are not free.

I have also seen headaches arise in those who resist the demonic spirit that is there, trying to squelch its effects without casting it out. So, constant headaches can be a result of a contest of wills between rival spirits within a person or between a person's will and a demon's will. As with Seansay, she had never directly invited demons to enter her, but by her determination to resist the desires of the generational spirits that had entered her at birth, she was suppressing the chief demon by her own strength of will. Because she wouldn't cooperate with the chief demon by becoming an addict, she suffered his attacks in ways she could not control: migraines and other unexplainable pains.

The Bible makes it clear that there is a hierarchy among demons and that there are "princes" of various geographical locations, as if they were given authority over all the demons in their region (see Ephesians 6:12). All demons have the same desire to kill, steal, and destroy as the devil, but because they live under a hierarchy, they are incapable of working and serving together as a unit. They do not serve the devil in love or joy, as the angels in heaven serve the Lord.

Though the devil is intelligent and crafty, he is also incredibly stupid and deceived. The fact that he challenged God and rebelled against him proves his stupidity, and his scheme to have the Messiah killed was his greatest defeat so far. Demons and the devil are blinded by their greed and are driven by their insatiable desire for more power to destroy. This coincides with the manner in which we see demons working in the lives of those who are suffering: When one "strong man" is challenged by another "strong man," greed does not allow them to peacefully coexist with one another, and the headaches that follow are a result of that conflict.

Growing Up with Headaches

My mother, Marianne, grew up with constant headaches. She was born into an abusive home where her father could not control his drinking or his temper. She went to bed with a baseball bat in case her father's violence turned against her and she had to defend herself. It was a terrible life of stress, and she was forced to pretend that all was well in front of the church community where he was an elder, meanwhile living in a secret hell most nights of the week. I have no doubt that demons from my grandfather entered into my mother to destroy her life in the same way, not because she deserved it or asked them to harm her, but because demons will force their way into the lives of anyone—through any door they can find, no matter how good or innocent that person is. But, like Seansay, my mother hated all she saw in alcohol. She was a very determined and loving person but, of her own admission, a very angry woman who refused to have anything to do with the abusive life she had lived as a child, and she wouldn't touch any kind of liquor because of it.

The day she first met my father, she said that she hated all men because of what her father had put her and her family through. She had resolved to live in a way that was right before God, honest and pure, and was fed up with the hypocrisy she saw in churches around her. Yet she was drawn to my father's sincere love for God and his dream of being a pastor, and when they married they longed to serve God as missionaries in Africa. Yet even in her faithful resolve to avoid alcohol and follow God, her headaches persisted. With each child she had, the headaches increased, and her twelve years of missionary service in Malawi—riding Land Rovers over the bumpy African dirt roads, enduring the incredible heat—forced her to spend days at a time on her back, unable to get up because of the pain. Because she was a determined woman who hated self-pity, she would force herself to cook and sew and care for all of us, but anger, pain, and frustration were always a part of her life.

Never did she or my father imagine that she could possibly have demons! For anyone in our family to even consider my mother to be oppressed by demons would have been sacrilege—she was a hero to us all. She loved the Africans deeply, she loved her family to the smallest detail, and above all she loved Jesus and was dedicated to Him until death. Many nights when she couldn't sleep because of the pain, she would lay awake in prayer or get up and read the Bible. She was a saint in our minds; yet she was so miserable in her pain and suffering. It seemed that her love for God and her commitment to serving Him as a missionary counted for nothing when it came to finding relief from her migraines and backaches. This sad experience of growing up and seeing my mother in intense agony from week to week convinced me at a young age that God does not do miracles today. If anyone was worthy of healing, according to my logic, she was. We all tried to rationalize her suffering as God's mysterious will, as somehow good for her, as a test, but never as something demonic to fight against with our faith.

Willpower Alone Is Not Enough

When my parents first learned about the power of God to perform miracles, to heal, and to cast out demons, my mother latched on to these truths and never let go. She asked for prayer to have her demons cast out, and she prayed herself to cast out whatever spirits might be inside of her, with no shame or fear. She was thrilled to finally have found the root of her problem and have someone to be angry at! We were a bit shocked to hear her speak so freely of how all her problems were because of demons in her life, but we couldn't ignore her healing and strength. Her migraines were gone, and though the devil tried to attack her in other ways, she was determined to see her victory. Years of trying to be a good Christian, serving God, refusing to live a life of sin as her father had—these were not enough to cast out the demonic force that had been in her life from the time she was a little girl. Only through strong prayers of deliverance did she find that freedom.

Headaches are so common that few people would consider them to be a result of demons. But these constant and unbearable headaches that block us from going forward in our lives, interfere with our relationships and jobs, and keep us enslaved to piercing pain are not a trivial matter. The devil and his demons are bent on causing suffering and stealing away whatever semblance of a life we may have, and if headaches can accomplish that, they will gladly use them. It is no coincidence that demons that vie for the head position in our lives create physical pain in our heads.

Obviously our head is an extremely important part of our body. Without it we couldn't survive—there is no such thing as a brain transplant! But not only is our head important in a physical sense, the Bible refers to the head in spiritual terms as well. Leviticus 26:13 speaks of how God set the Hebrew slaves free so that they could walk with their heads held high. Psalm 23 speaks of the Lord anointing our heads with oil. Isaiah 59 and Ephesians 6 talk of the helmet of salvation upon our heads and also upon the Lord's head. Proverbs 25 and Romans 12 say that God will heap burning coals upon the heads of the wicked. Deuteronomy 28 says that we who obey God will be the head and not the tail. Of course, we need to know that though each of us are different members of the Body of Christ, He alone is the head.

As demons struggle to become the "head" of our lives they may attack our physical heads, causing these constant headaches. Our response has to be—as always—cast them out. The Bible says that we should be transformed by the renewing of our minds in order to know God's good and perfect will. Though prayer, meditation, and reading of the Word are important parts of that transformation, there is more that we must do. We must use our faith to drive out whatever spirits are at work inside of us, causing whatever sort of pain or destruction. This is the only way we can become new creatures and testimonies of God's great power to deliver.

CHAPTER EIGHT

Spirits of Depression

Colleen was plagued with a spirit of depression. It caused her to lash out at those who loved her most, blaming her problems on her husband who loved her and supported her despite all the unhappiness in their marriage. When we first met her, she was considering leaving her husband, believing that there was no more hope of rekindling their love. She'd spend days at a time crying in bed with the covers pulled over her head, making her whole family worried and upset. Through the depression, other pains and physical problems arose that sent her to the hospital for surgeries that removed organs, but after each surgery new pains would arise from nowhere. Her husband urged her to see a psychiatrist when her irrational behavior became unbearable, and Colleen agreed that she needed help. But medication and psychotherapy had proven useless to her because her problems were demonic. She sought us out after seeing our TV program, but she didn't seem to have much hope that anything would really change.

When I prayed for Colleen and commanded the demons of depression to manifest, she began to scream at the top of her voice and grabbed her stomach as if someone had just stabbed her. Speaking in a low, hoarse voice, the demon revealed that it had been in her life since the time she was a small girl. It was the same demon of hatred and depression that had been responsible for her father's suicide and for the forty years of arguments and frustration in her marriage. The demon was stubborn and argued that it had a right to stay in her life because it had been there for so many years. But say what they want—demons must still get out in the name of Jesus when we use the authority given to us by God.

Colleen needed more than prayer; she needed a great deal of counseling, teaching, and encouragement to know that there really was a way out, that God was ready to do a miracle for her. Yet even so, prayer was the most important element of the deliverance process.

Depression is not always obvious. It can remain hidden in someone's heart for a long time, under a façade of a happy-go-lucky lifestyle, but eventually it creeps in and takes over all that a person loves and desires. There are countless medical explanations for depression, but its roots are spiritual more than anything else. People with the spirit of depression range from wealthy to poor, well-educated to illiterate, and can come from any culture or country on the globe. It is growing in numbers among Americans year by year. Some say this increase is due to the stigma of mental illness being lessened through education and, therefore, more people seek help for it. For whatever reason, the numbers of cases of depression in the U.S. has risen steadily in the past thirty years. Presently it affects more than nineteen million Americans, according to the National Mental Health Association (NMHA). Depression is the illness of this age.

The Underlying Causes of Depression

*"When my heart was grieved and my spirit embittered, I
was senseless and ignorant; I was a brute beast before You"*
(Psalm 73:21-22).

Demons of depression have been around for thousands of years, as long as evil spirits have existed. Trying to cure depression with therapy, support groups, and medication can bring some positive results; people with depression have been able to return to work, patch up their marriages, and families with that kind of care—yet only to a point. Slipping back into depression is always a risk, and constant dependence on therapy is the only way to cope, not knowing if another attack of depression is around the corner. Some people don't respond to medication or therapy at all and are left with no other option than to live with their disease.

Some of the common symptoms of clinical depression, according to the NMHA, are:

1. Persistent sad, anxious, or "empty" mood;
2. Sleeping too much or too little, middle of the night or early morning waking;
3. Reduced appetite and weight loss, or increased appetite and weight gain;
4. Loss of pleasure and interest in activities;
5. Restlessness, irritability;
6. Persistent physical symptoms that do not respond to treatment (e.g., chronic pain or digestive disorders);
7. Difficulty concentrating, remembering or making decisions;
8. Fatigue or loss of energy;
9. Feeling guilty, hopeless, or worthless;
10. Thoughts of suicide or death.

What makes depression so difficult for people to handle is that frequently there is no logical reason for it to exist. When a person with a good income, a loving family, and so many opportunities for the future suffers from depression, he can just appear to be an ungrateful slob who'd rather complain than be happy. People who suffer from these demonic attacks often rationalize their feelings, making themselves out to be victims who are treated unfairly by everyone around them and at times accusing those who love them of being unkind or uncaring. Because of that, they frustrate their family and friends, driving them away by their paranoid attitudes, and they become more alone and disliked than ever before. In this way, the demons of depression work hand in hand with the demons of division, creating isolation, loneliness, and misery.

I have prayed for many who have sought help in other churches, yet because these churches didn't know how to cast out demons or even identify the problem as demonic, the oppressed person left feeling angry with God because He "did nothing for them." Yet when the demons are tied up and cast out, these people's eyes are opened to see just how loving and great God is—and how eager He is to heal them and set them free.

Depression and the Lies of Satan

Although I have seen many become free and go on to live new lives, others just don't want to let go of their depression. They give up, preferring to hold on to the lie that their problem is just too big. A spirit of pride often accompanies depression, telling the person that no one else can understand their suffering, creating a smug and twisted sense of superiority. Deliverance requires humility and a confession that our problems are nothing compared to the power of the Lord. Some who have these demons of depression don't want to admit that their problems are on an equal par as everyone else's, and can be erased with the slightest move of God's hand. They prefer to imagine that their suffering is far greater, far more complicated than the ordinary person's. In such cases, they block their own deliverance until they come to the point of true humility before God.

God's love and power is so great, so amazing, and so ready to set us free that demons of depression stand no chance before our prayers of faith. But convincing those who are suffering from depression to believe in that truth is like trying to pull someone out of a deep, dark, slimy pit. Jesus said that our eyes are the lamp of our body. How we view our life and those around us determines our own inner health: "...if your eye is clear; your whole body will be full of light. But if your eye is bad, your whole body will be full of darkness. If then the light that is in you is darkness, how great is the darkness!" (Matthew 6:22-23). Yet even though spirits of depression keep people in such a great and overwhelming darkness, the oppressed person can choose to fight back, even if it is just a simple desire for freedom from deep within. If there are churches and pastors who are ready to fight along with them and give them the faith and the encouragement they need, they can break out and be completely set free.

Part of the deliverance process for those with demons of depression is to change their vocabulary. The final result for all of us is to have our thoughts and desires transformed by the Holy Spirit and to be made completely new, but a good first step is to be careful in what we say out loud. The tongue has the power of life and death (see the book of James), and by the fruit of our lips we can be filled with good things (see Proverbs 12:14). Because depression works solely with our thoughts and emotions, disciplining our tongue can have a great effect in reshaping our thoughts. The lies of the devil are the driving force behind this illness, and confessing words of faith and trust in God—in place of doubts and cynicism—are actually weapons to destroy the devil's hold on our minds. When Colleen stopped accusing her husband of treating her badly and not being a support to her and started to apologize for the wrongs she had done, their relationship changed drastically. When she went even further and began to lavish him with love, honoring him with kind words and support, she broke down age-old walls. Though they had been separated by all the anger and resentment on both sides, their love for each other was still alive. When she saw the change in him, it was much easier for her to understand that God truly does work through the words we speak (see Proverbs 15:4).

Organizations like the NMHA and other health care groups are deeply concerned about the victims of depression and have done extensive research and therapy to bring about a solution for these people. Their efforts are laudable and seem to be the only solution possible for those who have no faith in God. However, dealing with a problem that is demonic at its root with mere human intelligence and study is never going to bring about a total and permanent healing. That is something only God can do.

The word "depression" never appears in the Bible, but it is alluded to in various places: in Psalms, in Proverbs, in the story of King Saul and his fall from God's grace, in the suicide of Judas, and in the books of the prophets that speak of the despair and dismay of those who have rejected God's commands. In the twenty-first century, we see a kind of inward destruction that is becoming more prevalent as time goes by. Some would say that depression was just as widespread in the past but few people identified it. It could be true, but the Bible also shows us that as time goes on the evil in this world increases. Jesus asked His disciples one day, "...when the Son of Man comes, will He find faith on the earth?" (Luke 18:8). Faith and trust in God are slowly diminishing on this planet, and doubts and depression are on the rise.

Complete Healing Is Possible

When it comes to the power of God, the demons of depression, although they are able to destroy lives, are no different than any other evil spirit. The fact that so much literature and information on depression is available shouldn't cause us to think that depression is a problem on a higher level of "sophistication" or difficulty than others. That's completely untrue!

Some Christian psychologists have written about depression among Christians, and they have gone into great detail about therapies and procedures to overcome it. I think we like to imagine that, because of our advanced society, we have to deal with our modern day problems with doctorates alongside the Bible. But freedom from depression is much easier and straightforward than many Christians think. Spirits of depression need to be fought in a spiritual way, and we must cast them out in the same way as all other demons. As I've said before, prayers of deliverance are not magic formulas. Prayer can instantly heal a person's body and can instantly remove demonic spirits that once inhabited someone's life. But changing a person's entire way of looking at the world is something that each person has to choose to do himself. He must learn how to trust in God for all things. Through prayers of deliverance, the love and support of a church family, constant encouragement from the Word of God, and a lifestyle of communion with God, people who were attacked with demons of depression can truly be transformed by God's power.

For those who are suffering from depression, half the battle is knowing who the real enemy is. Depression can enter a life through many forms: the death of a loved one, loss of a job, rejection, fears, past abuse or neglect, uncertainty of the future—the list can go on and on. It's easy to blame other people or situations for the cause of depression, but depression is, at its root, demonic. It is a spirit that destroys a life from the inside out. But it absolutely can be overcome and cast out. Those who live under the power of this demon of depression see their world through a prism of doubt and negativity; to expect them to be happy and simply decide to have faith is unrealistic. They need people of God to lovingly care for them. They need strong prayers of deliverance to be set free. And they need God in His great mercy to begin to transform them so that they can begin to see the world through God's eyes rather than the devil's. With His eyes, their lives and hearts can be full of light.

> *"My heart is steadfast, O God, my heart is steadfast; I will sing and make music. Awake, my soul! Awake, harp and lyre! I will awaken the dawn...For great is your love, reaching to the heavens; your faithfulness reaches to the skies"* (Psalm 57:7-8,10 NIV).

CHAPTER NINE

Possessed Believers

Nancy was in her late twenties and had a good job in an insurance company. She had been blessed and healed in many ways during her six years as a believer. She had been a prayer counselor at a Pentecostal church, had spoken in tongues, and had been seen as a strong Christian woman.

But after five years she began to tire of her responsibilities in the church and gave up her place as a counselor. When I met her, she was abnormally quiet, withdrawn, rarely smiled, and found it hard to make any friends. At the end of meetings she would make a bee-line for the door. Though she often asked for help and advice, she rarely did what we suggested. At times when we pointed out a weakness in her life and warned her of the dangers of certain behavior, her reaction was to laugh sardonically—almost defiantly.

The first time we met with Nancy she told us that she had lately begun to be attracted to men, usually older married men from outside the church. Though these relationships had no future and were bound to make her unhappy, none of that seemed to matter. She was obsessed with having a man, any man, even though she admitted that she didn't like or trust those to whom she was attracted.

Finally, one particular day she opened up and began to explain. Her father had sexually abused her when she was a young girl. Her mother eventually found out but was afraid to confront her father and pretended like she didn't know what was happening. Then, when Nancy was fifteen, her mother demanded that she leave the house.

Now, even though years had passed, visiting her parents was a painful ordeal with overwhelming memories and unhealed wounds. Though she attended church, lust flooded into her mind and heart, and she felt unable to fight against them.

One night in the church the demons in Nancy manifested and made all sorts of threats. Sounds came out of Nancy's mouth that no person could ever invent. Horrible sounds. She vomited and wretched. Her tortured face and twisted hands were clear proof that something terrible was going on inside of her. I asked, "How long have you been here?" The demons growled, "Since before she was born! Why did you find me? She doesn't know I'm here. No matter what you do I'm not leaving!"

They said many other things during Nancy's deliverance. The demons inside of her said they didn't want her to ever get married or to have a normal, healthy relationship with a man; they were planning to make her sick and to have her commit suicide in the end.

This is not a crazy scene from a horror movie. This is something that the Lord Jesus saw and heard on a daily basis during His ministry. More than that, He dealt with people suffering from these types of problems and set them free. He always spoke directly to the demons, commanding them to leave and at times allowing them to respond. Sometimes they threw their victims on the ground, other times they screamed or interrupted meetings in the synagogue. But Jesus did not ignore the presence of evil spirits in people's lives.

Believers and Demons

Can a believer be oppressed or even possessed by demons? Yes. Nancy had been a faithful member of a church for six years; she thought she was baptized in the Holy Spirit, speaking in tongues and praying for others. But during the entire time she had been in the church, there were hidden feelings and desires from the past that had never left. Because the wounds of the past were not healed, evil spirits had a foothold in her life. She continually asked for forgiveness and prayed for Jesus to come into her heart and take away all the tormenting memories and desires from her mind. One day she confessed that she couldn't pray anymore because she felt like a hypocrite, as if a part of her longed for God but another part pulled her into sin and immorality.

Why is this? It's something that's explained again and again throughout the Old and New Testaments. In the time of the judges, the Israelites had conquered the Promised Land and were living there as the chosen people of God, but they frequently were overrun by their enemies and lived in misery and defeat. Similarly, during the time of the Lord Jesus, the Messiah was performing every kind of powerful miracle in front of the Pharisees, and even though they were the leaders of Israel, the chosen people of God, they killed Him. Just because we go to church and call ourselves born-again, Spirit-filled Christians doesn't mean that it's true. If we do not experience God's presence and live in His power, in truth we do not yet know Him.

It was confusing for Nancy. For years she had tried to be a good Christian and do everything right, but some hidden forces inside of her eventually came to the surface to destroy what little faith she had. When she finally came to us, she was ashamed and afraid. To some people the solution may seem to be ridiculously easy: just stop doing what is wrong and obey God. But Nancy had tried that, and the demonic desires that she hated were only suppressed, not cast out. Nancy's problem came from demons that had entered her life as a little girl, when she had been violently abused. She grew up feeling "dirty" and worthless, with a constant fear that people around her were planning to harm her the same way. When she first became a Christian, she threw herself wholeheartedly into the prayers and activities of her church, but no one took the time to discover that deep inside her heart lay dark and destructive forces. She hoped that through hard work and dedication to serving God these hidden issues would melt away. Instead, the harder she tried to ignore them, the more they grew until she collapsed in sin. Those evil spirits convinced her that someone as worthless as she was would never find a man who would treat her kindly and that since she had already been violated as a child, she had nothing more worth protecting.

Of course, we could never condone or excuse the sinful life that Nancy was living, but mere words of correction or exhortation were definitely not enough. Nancy was demon possessed. She heard their voices speaking to her in her mind, she felt an evil presence following her, and she was full of self-hatred and desperation. There is no possible way that Nancy had been baptized in the Holy Spirit, even when she had been speaking in tongues and praying for the sick. Baptism in the Holy Spirit is recognizable when all the fruits of the Spirit are evident in a Christian, and though they still are sinners in need of constant repentance, they take on the character of Christ. But Nancy only had a false appearance of Christian character while evil desires always tugged at her soul. The tongues that she spoke in were undoubtedly demonic.

Through a lot of care and encouragement, we were able to lead Nancy through a process of deliverance. When the demons in her manifested, they were stubborn and didn't want to reveal the horrible things they had done. They said there were seven of them and that they had been with her from the time she was in her mother's womb because of witchcraft in the family. They said that they wanted her to suffer, to be destroyed, eventually to die. They fought, roared, and vomited onto the floor. But no matter how strong they tried to appear, they had to kneel before the name of Jesus and confess their defeat.

Nancy's deliverance was not just a matter of one prayer or one experience of manifesting evil spirits. It took many prayers and much counseling for her to gain the strength and the faith to keep those demons out of her life. It wasn't because the power of Jesus wasn't strong enough or that our prayers were ineffective; I never allowed her to leave the church until every last spirit was driven out. But the weakness of her faith, her doubts, and her fears allowed the demons to return again by the next time we saw her. Just like the Bible says, evil spirits try to return to the house they once occupied (see Matthew 12:43-45). Every time we prayed for Nancy, we saw improvements in her life and in her character. Though the demons would return, the determination to fight back that grew in her heart, weakened their hold on her, and in time she was able to develop a solid faith in the Lord Jesus so that they were completely blocked from returning to her life.

Because Nancy was trying her best to find freedom and to give her life to the Lord, the process of deliverance took only two to three months. But had Nancy been unwilling to fight, the process might have taken longer or become bogged down in doubt and fear. That is why the *process* of deliverance is so important; it is not only one prayer. Every victim needs the love and care of his or her church until they find total freedom. However, willfully turning away from God after receiving deliverance is a serious and dangerous situation in which to be.

Today Nancy is absolutely free. With a new desire to love and follow God, it was easy for her to end her unhealthy romantic relationship with no fear or remorse—in fact, she felt relief and joy. Immediately she received an unexpected promotion on her job, and she found she was able to work with a clear mind and be pleasant to all her clients. Her face opened up into smiles and, at times, tears of joy because of what God had done for her. The voices and the demonic presence were gone, and, best of all, all of the pain and guilt of the past was healed. Because she was no longer torn between two worlds, Nancy could worship God and serve Him with a whole heart, and as she began to bear the fruit of the Holy Spirit in her life and change her character, she became baptized in the Holy Spirit and spoke in true tongues from God.

Possessed Believers

It has always been a common assumption that demonization was a phenomenon found only among unbelievers. Most, if they believed demons to exist at all, think they inhabit only the strangest people on the fringe of society—the mentally insane, the violent criminal, the Satanist, or occultist. But for those of us who have been involved in actively praying for spiritual deliverance on a regular basis, we are finding an alarming number of evangelical believers have evil spirits.

During our years of ministry around the world, the other pastors in our church and I have found a significant difference between the demons that manifest in people who are unbelievers and the demons that manifest in those who claim to be born again. The unclean spirits found hiding inside of believers are often the most terrible, violent, and complex—even worse than those spirits found in people involved in witchcraft and the occult.

Compared to those that work in people involved in witchcraft, demonic spirits in believers do not manifest easily. Casting these demons out is very tiring, not because the evil is too strong but because there is often resistance on the part of the believer. He refuses to accept the truth that he is actually demonized. These spirits choose to live in the minds and emotions of these people, and there they are able to resist challenges to their power in a much stronger way. Believers unknowingly give assent to the twisted logic of the demons as if it is the truth.

Believers who discover that they are under spiritual oppression react in different ways. Some are offended at the suggestion; they flatly deny that such a thing could happen to them because they have been active members of their churches for years, have felt the presence of God, and maybe even have spoken in tongues. Others are fearful that these evil spirits will destroy them since their faith up until that time has not protected them as they thought it should. Others, though it may sound hard to believe, even pride themselves as those who've been chosen to suffer more than the average Christian, even though it's demonic. It's something similar to a martyr complex. They hop from church to church, deliverance ministry to deliverance ministry, explaining in full detail the extent of their oppression and all the names of demons that other ministers found hiding inside of them. One particular lady who used to visit our church in New York would ask for prayer and, after receiving prayer for deliverance, politely suggest some new technique she learned from another pastor, urging us to try it too as we prayed for her! She really wasn't interested in finding her freedom—she just craved attention.

Fortunately, there are others who sincerely humble themselves before God and realize that their knowledge—their understanding of who God is and how the devil attacks—was not enough for them to block demons from entering their lives. Even if they were faithful church members, knowledgeable in the Bible, and honest in character, their "credentials" no longer matter to them; they just want to be free by the power of God. In this country, where diplomas and resumes mean so much, we like to hold on to proof that we are people who deserve recognition for what we've done. But a true Christian has no credentials and nothing to boast of—only the cross.

Examples from the Scriptures

There is a group of people who consider themselves Christian, who love Jesus, who want to do the will of God, who attend church faithfully, and who dream about the promises of the Bible coming true in their lives yet clearly have symptoms of demonization. Because of this, I cannot confidently say that everyone who is demonized would go to hell if they died at this moment. I've seen many sincere people who are trying to change and who are fighting against evil in the best way they know how; they are struggling to get free but are not yet there. I believe that if their life was taken at this moment, they would be saved because they recognized their need for God and the sacrifice of Jesus on the cross and they'd given their lives to the Lord Jesus, even though they hadn't yet overcome all the problems of the past. More often than not, the difference between them and a free Christian is just a matter of time.

One of the dangers facing possessed believers is laziness, allowing evil spirits to continue to work in their lives for an extended period of time. Some allow the oppression because they've never been taught that they can overcome it. Others simply don't want to change their lives. The longer people experience an unfruitful Christian life, the greater the temptation to be weak and indifferent toward the things of God because His promises are not coming true. With time, the tendency is for these people to grow increasingly colder toward God until they reach the point that they either fall away completely and lose their salvation or become unfeeling, apathetic, religious Christians. If by chance they don't fall away but turn into lukewarm Christians, their children, who see their weak and miserable lives, will seriously doubt whether faith actually works at all and may become either false and religious Christians as they had been taught or simply reject God altogether. "I know your deeds, that you are neither cold nor hot. I wish that you were cold or hot. So because you are lukewarm, and neither hot nor cold, I will spit you out of My mouth" (Revelation 3:15,16).

As discussed earlier, there are many instances in which Jesus and His disciples cast out evil spirits during their ministry. Two in particular happened in the synagogue. Let's look again at what happened while the Lord was preaching in a synagogue in Capernaum.

> *"They went into Capernaum, and immediately on the Sabbath he entered the synagogue and began to teach. They were amazed at His teaching; for He was teaching them as one having authority, and not as the Scribes. Just then there was a man in their synagogue with an unclean spirit; and he cried out, saying, 'What business do we have with each other, Jesus of Nazareth? Have You come to destroy us? I know who You are—the Holy One of God!' And Jesus rebuked him, saying, 'Be quiet!, and come out of him!' Throwing him into convulsions, the unclean spirit cried out with a loud voice and came out of him. They were all amazed, so that they debated among themselves, saying, 'What is this? A new teaching with authority! He commands even the unclean spirits, and they obey Him.' Immediately the news about Him spread everywhere into all the surrounding district of Galilee"* (Mark 1:21-28).

The man in this verse manifested an evil spirit in the middle of Jesus' teaching in the synagogue, which is no different than someone manifesting demons in the middle of a Sunday morning church service today! He was most likely a member of the synagogue; if not, he was a person seeking God, because he was in the synagogue on the Sabbath. Had anyone known he was demon possessed, they most likely would not have allowed an "unclean" person like that to worship together with them. Thus, we can assume that he was not an obviously demonized person but an ordinary looking man like the rest of the community.

Not everyone in the city of Capernaum attended the synagogue. There were people who didn't make the effort to go that day. But this man did, and, unexpectedly, the evil that had been inside of him manifested. Was this a cultural thing or merely something that happened in those days, when people were less educated? I think not. Why would the Holy Spirit record this incident in the Bible if it were not pertinent for us today?

Another passage is even clearer.

"And he was teaching in one of the synagogues on the Sabbath. And there was a woman who for eighteen years had had a sickness caused by a spirit; and she was bent double, and could not straighten up at all. When Jesus saw her, he called her over and said to her, 'Woman, you are freed from your sickness.' And he laid His hands on her; and immediately she was made erect again and began glorifying God" (Luke 13:10-18).

When the Pharisees complained that this miracle had been performed on the Sabbath, Jesus responded, "And this woman, a daughter of Abraham as she is, whom Satan has bound for eighteen long years, should she not have been released from this bond on the Sabbath day?" Jesus called this woman a daughter of Abraham! She was suffering terribly from the attacks of the devil, but in some way she must have been following in the footsteps of Abraham, the father of faith (see Galatians 3:6-9). Jesus didn't describe everyone as sons or daughters of Abraham; He knew that it was a description of faith, not merely ancestry. Jesus recognized that this woman had faith but at the same time was suffering under the oppression of the devil.

Though a believer may be convinced of the historical truth of the resurrection of Jesus and the existence of God the Father, he may still not truly know God. A person could believe that Jesus Christ rose again, but if it's only a logical or intellectual acknowledgment of fact, this victorious resurrection can bring no benefit to his life. He is not a new creature just because he gave up a few bad habits and changed his manner of speech. If others look at his life and see no difference between him and an unbeliever, if there is no power, no conviction, no passion for serving God, and if he reacts to problems in the exact same way as he always did—with fear and worry—then his "changed life" is nothing more than words and ideas.

A verse from the book of James describes this person's life accurately when it says, "You believe that God is one. You do well; the demons also believe, and shudder. But are you willing to recognize, you foolish fellow, that faith without works is useless?" (James 2:19,20). Believing that God exists or that the Lord Jesus rose from the dead is not enough; if we truly believe, we must act on our faith and live in servanthood to our Lord on a daily basis. In order to do that, we need to be in a close relationship of love and commitment to Him.

In the above examples, the man and woman had demons even though they were worshiping in the synagogue. We're not told what kind of believers they were. They may have been hypocrites, as the Pharisees, or living in some sort of sin; they may have been trying their best to follow God even though demons were attacking their lives. Whatever their situation, I am convinced the Bible includes their stories of deliverance to help us understand that even those who try to follow God can be bound by demons.

The Case of Judas Iscariot

Judas is another example. The disciple who betrayed Jesus to the chief priests and sent Him to His death is a hard case for many of us to understand. He lived day by day in Jesus' presence, saw the most amazing miracles, heard the most powerful messages and experienced the love and strength of the Lord for three years. He saw demons being cast out and the visible changes that occured when people were set free. He was even among those who were sent out to heal the sick and cast out demons, and they returned rejoicing that demons obeyed their commands. But something was seriously wrong. Jesus chose the twelve to be His close friends and disciples, but, even though He had chosen them, He knew that Judas was not free from demons. "Did I myself not choose you, the twelve, and yet one of you is a devil" (John 6:70). It was God's will for someone to betray the Lord Jesus, and Judas allowed himself to be used in that way.

But why didn't Jesus cast out Judas's demons if He knew they were there? Why couldn't He have been captured in a way that did not involve Judas? There are two reasons: God already had His master plan for the salvation of the world, and He is a just God. It is completely against the will and character of God to refuse help and freedom for those who seek it, and that is exactly what was lacking in Judas—a desire for help and freedom. Judas willfully chose to resist God's transforming power. Jesus didn't heal and deliver just anyone He saw walking down the road; He performed incredible miracles in those who came looking for Him. The Bible says that in Nazareth Jesus was unable to perform many miracles because the people could not believe that the carpenter's son they once knew was really the Messiah.

Judas's demon-possessed state was his own fault, yet he was able to deceive all the other disciples by appearing like one of them. He even performed miracles while demons were lurking in his heart. This is a scary concept. If the devil can counterfeit miracles in those he possesses, how will we ever know who is and who is not from God?

I'm sure Jesus used discernment to discover the true condition of Judas's heart, but there must have been many visible indications of the state of his heart. Judas's behavior and attitudes revealed that he was not a true disciple. The miracles were not proof of his righteousness, but his greed for money was proof of his demonic spirit. People often look at the signs and wonders that occur in churches— rolling in the aisles, gold dust falling from the ceiling, shaking, tongues, prophecies, etc.—and they immediately assume that the supernatural manifestations must be from God. But the fruit of the spirits that are causing these manifestations are many times not examined. If a ministry is involved in greed, gossip, immorality, false teachings, or other demonic symptoms, the supernatural signs are nothing more than demonic counterfeits. The spirit of Judas did not disappear with his suicide. I am convinced that if the Lord Jesus returned to earth in the same way He did two thousand years ago, plenty of demon-possessed "Christians" would reject and betray Him without thinking twice.

The Sons of Sceva

Acts 19:13-16 gives another example of believers who were demonized. This account of the seven sons of Sceva never says that they were demon possessed, but the fact that they were powerless before a single demon-possessed man shows that they were far from God and full of false teachings. Sceva was a Jewish chief priest, and his sons regularly went around performing exorcisms—rituals and incantations designed to drive out unclean spirits. They had heard of the power and authority to cast out demons that Paul and the other apostles had, and they decided to try it out. The seven of them commanded a demon to leave one man "in the name of Jesus whom Paul preaches." The demon mocked them, saying that it recognized Jesus and knew about Paul, "…but who are you?" With that the demon attacked and beat them, and they ran away naked and bleeding. They were religious men, most likely very good and moral men, based on their heritage, and they even had an appearance of faith in Jesus as they prayed in His name. But because they were devoid of a true relationship with God and the authority that only belongs to His followers, they were powerless before the devil and were shamed in front of everyone that day.

For Many Christianity Is an Act

Evil spirits use the knowledge of the Bible that a believer already has—combined with his pride in wanting to be recognized by his fellow Christians as "super holy"—and deceive the believer into thinking that the demons are not even there. Their crafty voices heap praise and adulation on the believer each time he attends a church service, memorizes special passages, organizes activities in his church, teaches a class and shows himself to be an expert on spiritual issues, or goes through some fleshly, emotional experience during a particular service. It seems to be a given that he is a wonderful servant of the Lord—a position and an honor that the believer covets.

Yet there is always something that doesn't quite fit in his life. Satan is there and in some way is stealing, killing, or destroying. It could be his marriage, his rebellious children, disease, failures in his job, depression, fears, addictions, anger, any number of things. But the logic of the devil always prevails, "You are a good Christian, but don't take all those promises in the Bible too literally. You've been chosen to suffer here on earth because you are so good and righteous. Of course you'll be blessed…in heaven when you die! Just keep on going. You're a hero to endure these problems."

It is not an easy job to help a fellow Christian who is truly suffering in this way. Issues of pride arise. The fact that they are under demonic oppression doesn't mean they haven't tried their best to do what is right or that they are evil people, and this becomes a very sticky point. I have seen destitute young men—who grew up poor, uneducated, addicted to drugs, and involved in crime—change their lives and, in time, become prayer counselors in the church. And I have seen upper-middle-class men—who have high-paying jobs and are upstanding members of their churches—come for help (privately, of course) because their lives were falling apart. The young men who were prayer counselors were perfectly capable of praying for and counseling the upper-middle-class men in the way that they needed, but because of the counselor's troubled past and lack of education, the men of higher social standing found it hard to listen to them. It's a pitiful example of the pride that most "good" Christians carry in their hearts. Even though I prayed for these men, the fact that they held themselves in such high regard blocked them from really being set free.

Fortunately, there are others who see that their education and financial status are worthless in the eyes of God, and they are willing to do whatever it takes to be free no matter how humbling or difficult. It is not easy for their egos to submit to strong prayers of deliverance, to be willing to manifest demons, and to follow the teaching and counseling from God's Word, but the freedom they receive is definitely worth it. Not only do they learn how to overcome their enemies, but they develop stronger characters of courage and humility through it all. With Jesus we are all the same, and in His eyes the beggar in Soweto is no different than the Sunday school teacher from suburban U.S.A. God is looking for hearts open to receive.

The only way a demonized believer can be set free is by breaking his pride, forgetting about the opinions of everyone around him, and becoming totally honest before God about his crippled life. Think about it: If just knowing the Bible was enough to overcome evil, then the devil would be a saint! Practicing the Word of God, not just knowing it, is what leads us to victory. In the Bible, Jesus is explained in simple and clear terms—the Living Water, the

Light of the World, the True Bread—and true freedom comes when we are simple and honest in our relationship with Him. He has the power and the desire to set us free, but we need to approach Him in humility and with a broken heart.

> *"For through the grace given to me I say to everyone among you not to think more highly of himself than he ought to think; but to think so as to have sound judgment, as God has allotted to each a measure of faith"* (Romans 12:3).

CHAPTER TEN

How to Be Set Free

Joanna had been involved in a cult for a short while, praying with them and participating in their ceremonies. As time went on, she became wary of their obsessive behavior and their demands on her to be just like them. She asked God to give her a sign, to show her if they were truly from Him, and in the next meeting she felt an evil force pick her up from her chair and throw her down to the floor. As soon as she could, she ran out the door. But when she was outside, she suddenly began to speak in tongues, something she had never experienced before. In her mind, the tongues were confirmation that leaving that place was the right thing to do.

Joanna acknowledged that such things as false tongues do exist, but she was convinced she had received the true baptism of the Holy Spirit that day. However, after this so-called "amazing" experience, the next several years of her life were wrought with hospitalizations, divorce, unemployment, and depression. I explained to her that it couldn't have been the Holy Spirit giving her those tongues; it was the same demons that had been destroying her life all along.

How could a person be so open to the work of demons that they're thrown to the floor one minute, then be so transformed by the Spirit of God that they receive the gift of tongues and are baptized in the Holy Spirit three minutes later ? Such a drastic change doesn't take place instantaneously. It requires time, not because God is unable but because baptism in the Holy Spirit involves much more than tongues and supernatural gifts. Baptism in the Holy Spirit begins with a willful choice to allow Him to change our character and our desires.

Bearing the fruit of the Spirit in our lives on a day-to-day basis is our proof of baptism in the Holy Spirit. It's a change that involves our determination to die to the flesh—combined with His supernatural grace to instill a new heart inside of us and empower us to perform miracles in His name. Only then are we able to use His gifts as He intended. And that, of course, takes time to develop. Even the first disciples had to earnestly seek and pray for the Holy Spirit to descend on them and prepare their hearts for Him to empower them. There is no doubt that salvation can come instantly to a person who is set free from demons that very same day—or even before their deliverance, as we've already said. But baptism in the Holy Spirit is not the same as salvation, and anyone who imagines that a demon-possessed person can immediately be baptized in the Holy Spirit moments after their demons are cast out has no idea of what the true baptism is. (Frighteningly, this idea is taught in many deliverance ministries today.)

Counterfeit Tongues and Miracles

Demons can speak in tongues and perform false miracles. They can manipulate events to appear as if they have the power to foresee the future. They know the details of your past because many times they were there trying to destroy your life in some way. They use these things to masquerade as the Holy Spiri, and since they know some of your inner secrets, they can appear to be the power of God.

In the book of Exodus, Pharaoh's magicians transformed staffs into snakes, just like Aaron had done. In Africa, mediums and witch-doctors speak in their own form of tongues during their seances and ceremonies. I have heard manifesting demons speak in false tongues, pretending that they are the Holy Spirit. I have heard demons laugh, saying that for many years they had fooled their victim into thinking that he or she was such a spiritual Christian, receiving "prophecies" and "words of knowledge" that were actually demonic. I never rely on a supernatural sign to determine whether or not someone is baptized in the Holy Spirit, but I look carefully at their character and their life of faith instead. I don't deny the existence or importance of true tongues and other gifts; to the contrary, I believe they play an extremely important role in the life of a Christian. But I also know that there is a great danger in confusing what is from God with what is from the devil.

The devil loves to deceive, to put on his favorite guise as an angel of light, and to confuse careless Christians. Casting out demons is more than a prayer or a decision. True freedom can only come by learning exactly who our enemy is and how he works—and in finding our Savior and realizing how abundantly He wants to bless us. If we accept the second rate "blessings" that the devil tries to offer as if they were from God, we'll always be confused and defeated.

Scriptural Examples

In the examples the Lord Jesus and His disciples give to us in the Word of God, we see certain guidelines for driving out demons and setting people free. The following are some observations:

1. Jesus gave direct commands to demons: be quiet, come out, never enter him again, etc. People who saw Him performing deliverances marveled that He spoke with authority and power and gave orders to demons (see Mark 1:25-27; Luke 8:29).
2. Jesus was always in control of the situation; demons were not allowed to do whatever they wanted. He asked questions of demons and relatives to gain information, and in one instance the demons had to ask Him permission to go into the herd of pigs (see Mark 5:9,13; Mark 9:21).
3. He addressed the evil spirit or disease directly. For example, "You deaf and mute spirit I command you, come out of him and never enter him again." His prayers were clear and specific

and were directed at the root of the problem. In the example of the daughter of Abraham, Jesus spoke to the infirmity that had been binding her up for eighteen years (see Mark 9:25; Luke 13:12).

4. Some demons manifested and others did not. In the nine specific examples of Jesus casting out demons, some demons spoke through their victims, others threw them to the ground or gave them convulsions, while others did not appear to manifest in their victims at all. But in all situations, the Lord Jesus did not lose sight of the fact that the root cause was demonic (see Matthew 8:28-32; 9:32,33; 12:22; Mark 1:24; 7:29; 16:9; Luke 9:42; 13:10-13; John 13:27).

5. Jesus and His disciples taught and counseled those that they set free, A man in the regions of the Gadarenes who had been demon possessed sat at Jesus' feet, clothed and in his right mind after his deliverance. Two chapters later Mary is doing the same, sitting at Jesus' feet listening to His teaching (see Luke 8:35;10:39).

6. Deliverance was simple and quick. There were no written prayers or ceremonies, nor did it take hours. He used His authority and sent the demons away.

7. Jesus cast out demons alone. When the twelve and the seventy-two were sent out (see Mark 6:7-13; Luke 10:1-20), they were sent in pairs and probably cast out demons alone (or, at the most, in pairs, but it is more likely that they followed Jesus' example). The only "team" that went around casting out demons in the Bible was the sons of Sceva, who got beat up and had to run away from the demons (see Acts 19:15).

8. Deliverance was done in public. Because of this, it was a powerful learning tool for everyone present. They saw the devil defeated, and they saw the authority of the man of God. Today, we may be too concerned about our image, too proud to accept this method of our Lord.

Exorcism and Empty Rituals

The word "exorcist" is defined as "one who employs a formula of conjuration for the expulsion of demons."[3] The Jews of the Old

Testament performed exorcisms that were elaborate rituals of incantations, a mix of faith in God with superstition. It was thought that evil spirits could only be cast out using these "magical" prayers and ceremonies. Interestingly, the Greek word that is translated "exorcist" appears only once in the Bible: when the seven sons of Sceva tried unsuccessfully to drive out demons.

> *"But also some of the Jewish exorcists, who went from place to place, attempted to name over those who had the evil spirits the name of the Lord Jesus, saying, 'I adjure you by Jesus whom Paul preaches.' Seven sons of one Sceva, a Jewish chief priest, were doing this. And the evil spirit answered and said to them, 'I recognize Jesus, and I know about Paul, but who are you?' And the man, in whom was the evil spirit, leaped on them and subdued all of them and overpowered them, so that they fled out of that house naked and wounded"* (Acts 19:13-16).

Jesus never performed a ritual to cast out demons; he had no written liturgy for the occasion that had to be read in just the right order. When He dealt with demons, Jesus used the spiritual authority He had to command them to leave. It was His faith that cast them out, not mystical words. This is the way that Jesus taught His disciples to cast out demons, and He expects us to follow His example by using the authority of His name.

The single time that the word "exorcist" was used in the Bible was to describe an attempted deliverance that was a complete and utter failure. The seven sons of a chief priest were using the name of Jesus as an empty formula, performing a ritual as the Jewish exorcists of the time were in the habit of doing. But instead of the demon being obedient and leaving the poor man, it beat up the seven brothers, tore off their clothes, and chased them out of the house. What a difference between this and Jesus and His disciples!

Yet, even today the Roman Catholic Church, along with other liturgical churches, continues to perform what they call "exorcisms." This is, in fact, an appropriate term for what they do because it's merely a collection of old, elaborate rituals and incantations.

Authorities on Catholic exorcism tell you that it's extremely dangerous to change the wording of the incantations because they'll lose their effectiveness. For demons that care nothing about the rights and wrongs of this world, it makes no sense to imagine that they would pay such close attention to the order of a written prayer! The rites of exorcism are more closely related to witchcraft than to the way Jesus and His disciples cast out demons.

In addition to this, those who perform exorcisms say that they lose a part of themselves each time an exorcism is done and that an exorcist is normally expected to live only fifteen years once he begins this ministry. Does this sound like Jesus and His disciples? If this is the truth, then demons are stronger than the Lord Jesus Christ. It's clear to me that the demons are not only working in the victim but in the one performing the exorcism, causing destruction in his life, too.

I have seen manifesting spirits hide themselves, pretending that they have been cast out, when in fact they were trying to deceive me or other pastors. If a false "prophet" or religion claims to exorcise demons and creates this aura of mystery through magical words and ceremonies, it's not too hard to imagine the devil deceptively playing along in order to create false ideas of who he really is and how he works. Our example should always be the Lord Jesus, and our authority should be based on His name, which is above all names in heaven, on earth, and under the earth.

Teachings on Deliverance—Which One's Right?

Almost any book on deliverance that you pick up will tell you that the first two things you have to do before starting any deliverance is to find a private room and form a team of between two and six people. Strangely, Jesus did neither.

Private or Public?

There were times that Jesus hurried up and cast out demons as He saw crowds approaching, but His deliverances and healings were public. Some argue that it's because He had no building or church, but in the example of the healing of Jairus's daughter, He created a private place where there would only be men and women of faith.

He could have done that at other times but clearly chose not to. Of course, that doesn't mean we shouldn't cast out demons privately, but we also shouldn't make a law that it has to be done privately when the Bible does not teach that.

There are millions of Christians who don't even believe that demons exist simply because they've never seen one manifest. These same Christians wouldn't know what to do if they did come face to face with a manifesting demon because they've never seen a deliverance. I know this because I used to be one of these Christians! I was a pastor's son who had no idea that demons really existed, much less how to fight them. I had read the Bible from cover to cover a number of times, I had been to church every Sunday of my life, but I had no idea what to do if confronted with an evil spirit. Finally, at age twenty-seven I was in a meeting where pastors were casting out demons in a deliverance service, and my eyes were opened. Ever since, my experience with Jesus has been different. What was crucial to opening my eyes was seeing the demons manifesting and being cast out *publicly*. As I watched, I learned that evil really existed—and that those who live by faith have the power to overcome it.

When a pastor friend of mine in Brazil first found Jesus, he was in a meeting where a particular demon manifested and declared who he was. A shock went through my friend's body because that was the spirit he and his family made offerings to in spiritism, and it was known to be very strong. He knew it was that same spirit because he'd seen it manifest in the "centros" of spiritism, and here in the church it was speaking and acting in the same exact way.

The demon threatened to make the pastor sick and to kill him. But during the deliverance the pastor told the people in the church, "If this demon has power, I'll die or become sick within a few days. But if Jesus Christ has power, the demon will leave, this man will become free, and nothing will happen to me. Come back in three days to see if I'm sick or dead."

My friend was dumbfounded. He hadn't thought of going back to the church, but after that he couldn't wait to go back and see what happened to the pastor. He went each day for the next three days and sat on the front row, watching the pastor. He especially watched the pastor's legs because this spirit was known for causing terrible sores on legs and feet and making people crippled. When my friend saw that the pastor did not get sick and that the name of Jesus really did have power over the strongest demons, he gave his life to Jesus!

Alone or in Teams?

The other point that many deliverance teachers make is that there must be a deliverance team. In my experience, when you ask someone to help you it's a sign of weakness to the demons and they get even stronger. One person with the authority of Jesus Christ is more than enough to cast out any demon, no matter how strong. If I have the authority of the Lord Jesus Christ, and I have been called to carry on His work in this world, I have everything I need, in His name, to stop the work of the devil. At times, however, a demon can be extremely violent and have superhuman strength, and the help of other strong men is often needed to hold the person so the demon does not hurt him. I have seen manifesting spirits try to throw people off the altar or smash their heads onto the floor or wall, so help from other pastors and prayer counselors to restrain them can protect them from harm.

Some authors advise one or two team members to speak in tongues throughout the deliverance, one to read the Bible, one to write down everything that is said, and one to stand by in case the main person doing the deliverance gets tired. But the Bible never teaches any of this! Many times these people take hours to set one person free or, at times, have to stop and come back the next day to finish the job. This is not biblical. We've been deceived and have turned something easy into something extremely complicated. Other pastors and I have been involved in prayers for deliverance morning, afternoon, and evening on a daily basis for many years (I myself since 1987), and in my experience, if we do it exactly like Jesus did, it works!

What's Important?

We have to be careful not to mix up the physical and spiritual aspects of deliverance. At times people vomit when demons are cast out, even vomiting up food or objects that had curses placed on them. I have seen amulets and pouches full of herbs from witchcraft vomited up. In Brazil it's common for needles and glass to be vomited up during prayers. In Portugal it's common for people to start burping loudly during deliverance. But not all demons come out this way; even after vomiting and burping some people continue to manifest spirits.

Some people teach that demons leave a person only through the mouth (or one of the other orifices of the body) and that if a person is speaking or singing during the deliverance the demons will not be able to leave because the way is blocked. There is no biblical basis for saying that evil spirits need a physical opening to leave the body. Demons are spirit. When Jesus released the daughter of the Syrophoenician woman, she was at home when the deliverance happened. No one was there to encourage her to cough or sneeze or breathe heavily so that the spirits would leave, as some teach today. With this kind of logic we would all recommend that our church members make sure they keep their ears, eyes, and noses taped shut to keep demons from flying in!

This preoccupation with the physical is unnecessary. What determines the freedom of a demon-possessed person are the faith of the one performing the deliverance and the behavior of the freed person after the deliverance. Physical orifices have no bearing on whether evil spirits enter or leave a person; that is determined by who they have in their heart. I agree that the person receiving deliverance should remain quiet and not sing or pray, not because they need to keep their throat clear but because they need to concentrate on the deliverance.

The Sacrifice of Being Involved in Deliverance

Another false teaching, which unfortunately seems to be considered common knowledge, is that those who enter the deliverance ministry will suffer terrible demonic attacks and be unable to live a normal life because of this very difficult calling. Authors of various books seen on the shelves of Christian bookstores claim that, because they are on the front lines of spiritual warfare, they have to deal with Satanic visions, they cannot marry or have children, or they have to suffer some incurable disease as they "stand in the gap" for those who are demonized.

This is ridiculous and unbiblical! I can't count the number of demons my wife and I have cast out—much less all the other pastors I have worked with through the years. I have preached directly and emphatically against those who practice witchcraft in churches and have raised the anger of the local African churches that mixed spiritism with Christianity. Witches have made sacrifices against me and other pastors, intent on destroying our churches and our lives, but I have never even once experienced the sort of torment that these authors do. My wife and kids are happy, healthy, and blessed, as are the families of the pastors I know. Persecution is a normal part of our lives, but we are in no way tormented or held back by demons!

The same Lord who casts out the demons as I pray is the One who places His loving arms of protection around all of us. But if I ever become foolish enough to turn my back on Him, I can be sure that the devil will gladly use that small opening in my life to destroy me after all those years I spent fighting against him. The only conclusion I can make about those who are involved in spiritual warfare but are also under oppression is that they themselves are demonized and don't yet know the fullness of God's presence in their lives.

We all are called to fight in this battle against the work of the devil in our lives and in our families and friends. Every church has the obligation to teach its members how to overcome in our fight, which means that every church should be a deliverance ministry—along with the other ministries of preaching, teaching, community outreach, missions, healing, praise, and worship that God has called His Church to perform. No one has to suffer torment from the devil just because he prays against him. Each one who learns how to put on the full armor of God and go on the offensive can see much greater fruit in his life than those who wish to stand on the sidelines. Just as Jesus and His disciples treated setting people free from evil spirits as an ordinary part of their lives, so should we.

The Authority We Have

When praying to cast out evil spirits, it is extremely important for the one who is performing the deliverance to be in close communion with God. As in the example of the seven sons of Sceva, the demons could say the same thing to us: "I recognize Jesus, and I know about Paul, but who are you?" Faith to fight against the devil starts first and foremost with our relationship with Jesus as our Lord and Savior. Without that, we have no authority and no rights as His children. Our daily obedience to Him and our daily awareness of how hopelessly lost we are without Him will keep us close to our Father in heaven. He is our lifeline. Jesus warned the disciples not to rejoice just because they had seen demons obey their words but to rejoice because their names are written in heaven. We also need to keep our eyes on our own salvation and not imagine ourselves powerful when demons submit to us. In fact, they do not submit to us at all—they submit to our Lord who dwells in our hearts.

We must also remember that demons have already lost the battle. They have to come out in the name of Jesus Christ, and that is that! We can't engage in debates with a manifesting spirit who is trying to convince us that he is too strong for us. Demons have to shut their mouths because they are all liars, and they have even deceived themselves into thinking they are stronger than they really are. We who have Jesus in our hearts and the truth of the Word of God in our minds don't have to worry about how strong or clever spirits may appear. We never have to run away from a manifesting spirit.

Some people who have evil spirits in their lives do not manifest them; because of fear, pride, or doubts, they don't want to let the demons out. We can pray for them, but because they are trying to hold the demons inside, they cannot be completely freed—even though they may see some changes in their lives from the prayer. Sometimes it takes a while for people who are suffering from evil spirits to soften their hearts enough to allow them to come out. Other people who are oppressed may not manifest when they are delivered; they have given their lives so completely to Jesus and want to serve Him so much that the spirits who tormented them before are made weak and leave easily without a fight.

Fighting the power of the devil that is at work in people around you doesn't mean you have to drag them into church or force them to manifest; there is a good chance you won't be able to do either! But prayers of power against the evil spirits that are attacking you through others are effective and necessary for all of us. If your boss is oppressed with the spirit of anger and keeps the workplace in an atmosphere of tension and fear, you who belong to Christ have the ability to pray against the work of those spirits. Maybe through him you began to have sleepless nights and were terrified of going to work each day. Perhaps your ability to do your job was affected, and because of that you got into more trouble or were overlooked for a raise. The spirits oppressing him moved on to oppress you.

We Have to Fight!

Many Christians today don't understand spiritual warfare. If you pray, "Oh Lord, please help me. Please make my boss change. Please don't let him get mad at me today," you are going to be disappointed when you see no change. It's not because God doesn't want to help you—He wants to change the situation more that you do. But He's waiting for you to pray with real faith, to stand up and fight the spiritual battle you are in.

In your prayers, you have to get angry—not at your boss, but at the demonic forces at work in him that are trying to destroy your life. You have to speak directly to the evil spirits attacking you and command them to get away from you, ordering them to be bound up by the power of the Lord Jesus. As you pray with conviction in your heart, God will give you the words to say. God has given us many passages that describe destroying our enemies and making them bow before us. Those enemies are the spirits of darkness who we have to hate and grind under our feet! By hating the devil, we love God; by fighting against the spirits of darkness at work in your boss (or anyone else in your life who is oppressing you), you are doing a kindness to him that can eventually set him free.

Deliverance and spiritual warfare need to be a regular part of our lives. Those who know they are suffering from spiritual attacks need to begin praying right away for their freedom. They need to find a church that knows how to deal with these problems and fight until the evil spirits are gone. They need to be counseled in how to be truly saved and filled to overflowing with the Spirit of God. And they need to continue in the battle. Those who are free are not exempt from the fight. Along with praying for others in need, we have to pray daily against all attacks the devil may try to bring our way—even before they come—binding up evil spirits that want to block us, our families, and our country, from receiving God's blessings. We can't stop fighting until the day we die. But if we fight with faith, we will win every battle, because Jesus brought us victory on the cross.

Lindi

Lindi's marriage began deteriorating almost as soon as she and her husband got married. They both drank heavily and fought constantly. During these bouts of anger, both she and her husband would throw whatever they could get their hands on: plates, glasses, pots—anything. One day her husband picked up a hatchet and started swinging it around wildly, trying to kill Lindi. Almost every night after that it was the same thing. Once, he actually hit her in the back with the axe and continued to punch and kick her until she was unconscious. That night Lindi almost died. Every house they lived in had holes in the walls and the doors from the axe.

When she came to the church, the pastor had everyone stand up to pray for their problems. He said, "Fight against your problems!" Lindi thought, "Now, that's one thing I know how to do. But what does he mean? How do I do that in the church?" But as she watched the people around her rebuking their problems by faith, identifying them and refusing to accept them, she joined them. She flailed her arms around, inadvertently hitting the man next to her, but fighting the devil with all her might. After that prayer she felt completely different.

Within weeks she was promoted in a job where promotions had been an impossible dream for her, and she was able to forgive her husband. Thinking back on those times she can't understand why she didn't leave her husband, but she just didn't think of it. The spirits of violence and poverty have been gone for more than nine years now, and anyone who knows Lindi cannot imagine that she ever was a violent, oppressed woman. She is known for her kindness and patience.

CHAPTER ELEVEN

Faith without Intelligence

Just as intelligent faith is powerful and able to change the impossible for the glory of God, faith without intelligence is ineffective at best, dangerously heretical at worst, and, either way, brings shame to the name of Christ. The world is already familiar with plenty of scandals, lies, and tragedies involving church leaders. An obvious example are the various sects who prophesied the exact date of Christ's return, waited patiently as the hours ticked by, and went home looking like fools. Most people who made themselves famous by an unintelligent faith were zealous, hard-working, and dedicated. But if their faith is unbalanced, unbiblical, and fleshly, all the hard work is for nothing. "Unless the Lord builds the house, they labor in vain who build it" (Psalm 127:1).

"Leave your mind at the door" and "Don't think, just believe" are examples of the misguided notion that faith and intelligence are incompatible. These statements are sometimes heard in charismatic churches, and I can understand, to a point, why they might say such things. Western culture has been so steeped in a rational, analytical assessment of everything we eat, see, and hear that the voice of God is often drowned out by our logical demands for empirical evidence. Faith is not faith if we don't believe without seeing, but it doesn't mean that we turn off our minds. It means that our minds are used in a godly and spiritual manner, understanding the way the spiritual world works, as God shows us in the Bible.

Intelligent faith doesn't mean that faith is only for intellectuals, theologians, and scholars. The intelligence that God intends for us to use is not academic but one that understands who He is by His promises. It is a faith made alive by a personal relationship of commitment and submission to Him. It's a faith that anyone can have regardless of mental acuity or education. It comes from an innate knowledge deep within that God exists and rewards those who love Him, from the poorest child to the most famous business mogul. Our God-given common sense helps us to step back from our problems, look at who our Father in Heaven is, and assess our lives based on what we know is holy and true—whether we fully understand it or not. It's not reasoning based on scientific discoveries or even on church history and past events, but on the unchangeable and eternal Word of God.

False Prophets and Dubious Prophecy

God has made clear in the Bible that false prophets are those who claim to speak for the Almighty and yet prophesy lies. The New Testament, from Matthew to Revelation, warns against false teachers and prophets. The false prophet in Revelation shares in the same punishment as the beast when the final judgment comes. God has always seen false teachers and prophets as people who do what is evil, so much so that the Old Testament commands them to be put to death! Although the many laws of the Old Testament have been made unnecessary in this age, God's attitude on false prophecy throughout the ages is very clear: it is no different than idolatry.

"But the prophet who speaks a word presumptuously in My name which I have not commanded him to speak, or which he speaks in the name of other gods, the prophet shall die.' You

may say in your heart, 'How will we know the word which the
Lord has not spoke?' When a prophet speaks in the name of
the Lord, if the thing does not come about or come true, that is
the thing which the Lord has not spoken. The prophet has spo-
ken it presumptuously; you shall not be afraid of him"
(Deuteronomy 18:20-22).

Churches that believe and practice prophecy as a supernatural
gift often find themselves in the predicament of acknowledging that
some of their leaders or "prophets" are not always getting it right. In
fact, few claim to have 100 percent accuracy in their prophesying,
but no one seems to be concerned that they sometimes are receiving a message from a spiritual force other than God. Prophecies and
"words of knowledge" abound in such numbers that Christians in
these movements have shifted from a gospel based on the Word of
God to a gospel of whatever the prophet of the day has to proclaim
about their lives.

It is intoxicating to feel that God Himself has chosen to speak
specific messages to you alone and to reveal His particular plan for
your life. It's a great ego boost to know that God has singled you
out. No matter how hard you read the Bible, you know you'll never
find the name of the city you should move to (unless it's in the
Middle East) or the exact name of the person you're supposed to
marry, but ministries that promote prophecy are attractive because
they seemingly provide a short cut to God.

Evelyn experienced false prophecy a number of times in her life
when she was feeling alone and unsure about her future. They were
beautiful words, and some even spoke of things in her past that she
had shared with no one else. She was absolutely convinced that they
were from God, and she felt tremendous joy and elation after each
one. But from that point on, the Bible seemed dull and irrelevant
for her.

The summer between her freshman and sophomore years in
college was a crossroads for her. Having left the safety of home on
the mission field in Korea, where her parents still worked, she was
unsure of what direction to take in her life. She determined to transfer out of the insulated Christian environment of Seattle Pacific

University to "see the world" and move closer to New York City, where she believed she would learn to be tough and survive anything. But while taking her summer break with family members in the Midwest, she felt confused and unsure of diving into the unknown so far from home. She had been accepted into Rutgers University in New Jersey, but she felt that she might be making a terrible mistake.

The elders of her church gave her various prophecies encouraging her not to be afraid. They said many comforting words, but they were also very vague. She transferred to Rutgers and suffered one of the worst years of her life. In hindsight she knows that God was urging her through common sense to go home to her parents for a time, to work, and to pray about her future before continuing college. But her stubbornness and embarrassment at the thought of running back home, in combination with the prophecies she received, pushed her to make one of the greatest mistakes of her life.

If God truly had been speaking to her through prophecies that summer, why didn't He guide her in the right direction? God is faithful and loving, He helps us even when we live by our own flesh, and He hears our cries when we fall on our face. The following year Evelyn became actively involved in the InterVarsity fellowship at school and began to "hear" God again through the studying of His Word. But it wasn't until after the devil had attacked her in ways that took her many years to overcome.

Elation and Frustration

There are churches that are so entangled in the plethora of "prophecies" that erupt after revival meetings or apparent "outpourings," that members who are told they have a special anointing to perform specific ministries leave the church in anger because they think the leadership fails to recognize their new calling. Prophecies that fizzle out after the initial wave of excitement leave the members with more frustration than faith. After a prophecy is proclaimed, the common advice given is, "Put it on the shelf and wait for confirmation." They might as well be saying, "Maybe it's from God, and maybe it's not. Maybe it was just the overzealous imagination of the pastor, or maybe it just came straight from the

devil. Wait and see if a confirmation appears." I understand that the
Bible tells us to test the spirits, but the idea that the church could be
an open venue for demonic words to be mistaken for God's word
should be completely unacceptable.

Prophecy is not an unbiblical practice; the Bible is made up of
prophecies and historical accounts that are combined in the perfect
plan and inspiration of the Holy Spirit. The apostle Paul exhorts us
to seek the gift of prophecy to build up the church (see 1
Corinthians 14). The prophecies that foretold future events in specific detail were given for the writing of the Scripture, to be pre-
served until the last days to warn, comfort, and encourage all
believers through the ages. Other prophecies were words of instruc-
tion and teaching that came from the Holy Spirit, both before and
after the coming of the Messiah, to edify God's people.

King David wrote in the Psalms that the Lord is our shepherd
and leads us to green pastures. It was a prophecy written for us—to
hold on to, to claim, and to believe in during difficult times. Paul
wrote that if we submit ourselves to God and resist the devil he will
flee from us; this is another prophecy that will come true if we
believe and practice it. While these words came directly from God
to us, they also came through the intelligent faith of the men who
wrote them down.

Dealing with prophecy today needs to be done with great care.
If God hates false teachers, it would be wise to be cautious of accepting any and every prophetic word that we hear. In many charismatic
churches today, it is common for two or three (or more) church
members to speak out during the worship time, speaking as if their
own voice was the voice of the Lord, sometimes ending their
prophecies with a solemn, "Thus saith the Lord!" If the Lord is
speaking so supernaturally, revealing specific directions, times, and
places of His plans for us, are we supposed to treat it with the same
authority as the Word of God? If His prophetic word is being spoken, then what place does the Bible take in our lives? Are His revelations today just as much His word as the Scriptures that were
written down thousands of years ago? Can God actually say some
things that are "sort of" important while other things are *really*
important?

The common attitude in some churches is to wait and see if a prophecy really is true—to "put it on the shelf." If what is said does not directly contradict the Bible and seems like something good and edifying, most church leaders willingly accept the prophecy as from God, but they allow a possibility that it may not have been real, that only time will prove its truth. In other words, leeway is given to those who boldly proclaim to be God's direct mouthpiece, in consideration that maybe somehow they got it wrong. But if "prophets" are making mistakes, how are churches dealing with these so-called men or women of God? Maybe the next time these people are not listened to as closely, but I'm not aware that churches are disciplining or silencing or treating them seriously as Jesus would have done to a false prophet. Prophecy has become a vague and subjective thing.

Dreams, visions, and word-for-word communications from God are easily counterfeited by demons. They are popping up in churches all over the country every week. If God is communicating His will and direction in such detail to so many people, why aren't more miracles happening that transform the nation? Why are so few people responding to God's call to "go and make disciples of all nations"—to save lost souls in places such as Eastern Europe, Asia, and Africa, where people are dying under the weight of poverty, oppression, witchcraft, AIDS, and other deadly diseases? If God chose to give His specific and direct words to the affluent and apathetic Christians that populate the United States, I would imagine they would be words of discipline, correction, and wrath toward their self-centered lives, not the kind of prophecies that urge believers to just "celebrate" and "be refreshed."

Witchdoctors, fortune-tellers, and mediums regularly give prophecy that are straight from the mouth of demons. Seers can tell you about your past and your future, or pass on "messages" from dead relatives—even things that only you and your relative could possibly know about. But the source of all these supernatural revelations is demonic. Just because a prophecy speaks of some hidden secret that you alone know doesn't mean the word is from God. The same deceiving spirits that work through mediums work inside the church, spreading the subtle lies of the devil. Some prophecies are demonic and others are just people offering their own opinions and ideas, cloaking them in an aura of direct revelation, as if it were truly from God. However it happens, these things are used by the devil to deceive and block people from really knowing God's will for their lives.

Empty Enthusiasm

The editor of Charisma magazine wrote a telling editorial in its May 2001 issue:

> "It's time to get off the floor. How many times do we need to be slain in the Spirit before we will begin sharing the gospel with our neighbors and coworkers? How many more doses of the anointing do we need before we will go out into the harvest where the Lord is waiting to demonstrate His power? How many prophecies do you need to receive before you will believe you are called to minister? Please stop hiding inside the church. God knows the lost aren't going to come in that uninviting building, so He has already gone outside to look for them. So should we."[4]

If the result of so much prophecy, shaking, and falling on the floor is apathy toward the lost, what kind of spirit is manifesting here? If salvation and evangelism are relegated to a back burner, just for a chosen few, the gospel of Jesus Christ truly has been sold out for a cheap counterfeit. Jesus' final command was not just for the disciples to go through all the world and preach the gospel; it was a command to all who are His followers. When there is no fruit in a church it becomes clear that the signs and wonders that exist are, in fact, false.

When Peter spoke boldly to Jesus, saying that he would not allow Him to enter Jerusalem, they appeared to be words of love and faith. But Jesus was not fooled by the words of the devil coming through the mouth of his friend, and Jesus rebuked him by saying, "Get behind me Satan!" The spiritual appearance of a Christian leader is too often confused with true spirituality, just as the "angel of light" is so often confused with the Light of the World.

I've counseled many people who are clearly demonized but are experiencing all sorts of prophecies and visions. They're convinced that they have a "great ministry," but at the same time their lives are falling apart! This, just as most of what we see in churches today, is the work of the flesh at best, and demonic at worst. The Bible teaches about prophecy and the guidance of the Holy Spirit, and these things are absolutely necessary for us to walk in the mighty power of God. But what's happening today in churches all over America is not from God; if it were, people and churches would be turning the world upside down. Hospitals would be emptying and prisons would be full of transformed men and women. Instead of guiding people to a true knowledge of God and a life of sacrifice, prophesies today are used to ask for offerings on TV or to work the congregation up into a frenzy of emotion.

Falling under the Power of What?

There are Christians who argue about whether or not miracles, healing, and speaking in tongues exist today. But no matter what side of the debate they're on, everyone who believes in the Bible agrees that these things did exist at one point in time. No Christian denies that miracles, healing, casting out of demons, and speaking in tongues really occurred in the first century church; from Scripture these facts are undeniable. However, when it comes to being "slain in the Spirit," there cannot be any similar agreement because there are no clear examples of it in the first century church.

The phrase "slain in the spirit" does not appear in the Bible, nor is the phenomenon clearly mentioned in any way. James 5 speaks about anointing with oil and healing the sick. Acts 3 speaks about the apostles being baptized in the Holy Spirit and speaking in tongues. First Corinthians 14 deals with tongues, the interpretation of tongues, and prophecy, and how they fit into the working of the church. Yet nowhere in Scripture are there examples of being "slain" like what is practiced in churches and revival meetings all over the world. There is not one account in the Bible of someone receiving the Holy Spirit and being knocked backwards to the floor in a swoon. Not one apostle laid his hand on the head of a believer expecting them to fall unconscious, much less with special ushers ready to catch them.

If this is such an important work of the church, as many evangelists emphasize, why wasn't it established in the New Testament?

If there was a time for being "slain in the Spirit," it was surely the day of Pentecost. There was the sound of a rushing wind and what looked like tongues of fire on everyone's head, and they were filled with joy as they began to speak in tongues. But, strangely, no one was "slain." Instead of falling on the floor unconscious, they went out and saved thousands of souls. Was the anointing not so strong that day as it is today? When Cornelius received the baptism in the Holy Spirit there is no mention of being "slain." In the first believer's baptism in the Spirit, as well as the first Gentile's baptism, being "slain in the Spirit" is conspicuously absent. How can it now be the central element in certain ministries?

I've spoken to some who have visited revival crusades where hundreds and thousands were "slain" by a wave of the hand of the preacher. Crowds topple over like dominos, stand up, and topple over again. It is considered proof that God is moving there, and followers boast to each other about how many times they were "slain," as if it were a sign of greater spirituality. There are a few churches in Ghana that keep a well-stocked first aid kit on hand to bandage up all the wounded church members who fall over in the service. The more band-aids you have when you leave, the greater the respect you earn in the church!

This phenomenon of being "slain in the spirit" became common in the mid-nineteenth century with the rise of the holiness movement and Pentecostalism, and it has been accepted by many to be a sign of the anointing of God. Lately it has taken on new dimensions, and, to all appearances, it is an absolute requirement for the followers of certain ministries to fall over at meetings. Some pastors are seen throwing the Holy Spirit around like a pitcher throwing a baseball as their congregations eagerly comply by falling down. Is this the way the Lord Jesus or the apostles treated the Holy Spirit? Was He ever used to excite a crowd to an emotional frenzy?

"Slain in the Spirit" adherents cite Paul's experience on the road to Damascus as a biblical example of this practice. But what happened when Paul fell? God was strongly rebuking him for his sin, and Paul was punished by blindness until he humbled himself before the Lord Jesus. He had been an enemy of the gospel and was full of demons of hatred and violence, so much so that he was going to Damascus to throw believers into prison. His experience was certainly not one of ecstasy and anointing in the Holy Spirit. Though it was a turning point in his life that prepared him to receive Jesus into his heart three days later, it was nothing like the experiences of being "slain" that are occurring in churches today.

Some cite the Mount of Transfiguration as an example to explain being "slain." Elijah and Moses appear together with Jesus in a glorified appearance, shining like the sun with clothes as white as the light. A bright cloud overshadows them and God's voice speaks, telling the disciples, "This is my beloved Son in whom I am well pleased, hear Him!" With this, the disciples fall on their faces in fear. Some consider the cloud as being the anointing of God, that when He is close to us we lose our strength and our senses as if we are in a cloud.

However, the apostle Peter speaks of how they were eyewitnesses of Jesus' glory and heard the voice of God emphatically stating that indeed Jesus was the Son of God (see 2 Peter 1). For Peter, the affirmation from God the Father that Jesus was the Messiah was the most important thing that happened on that mountain. He makes no comment whatsoever about a wonderful experience of falling down! It was just a natural reaction of being faced with such an extraordinary sight. The unique event at the Mount of Transfiguration was in preparation for the most powerful and life-changing event in the history of the world—the death and resurrection of the Lord Jesus.

We can be sure that an appearance of Jesus in glory will not happen again until He returns. To use this story to legitimatize the falling over of Christians in churches today is to cheapen the importance of what happened on that mountain. There are four accounts of the Mount of Transfiguration in the Bible: in Matthew, Mark, Luke, and 2 Peter. Yet only the Gospel of Matthew mentions that they fell. The others pay no attention to it. If being "slain" is an important spiritual experience, why didn't Mark, Luke or Peter even mention it? And if being "slain" is as important as so many ministries claim, it would have been clearly taught in the Bible.

Today, some of the greatest truths are being taught by spirit-filled churches that recognize the place of the Holy Spirit in a Christian's life; yet some of the most dangerous deceptions are also being taught by the same people. We need to be aware that wherever there is truth that sets men free, the devil will attempt to come with his counterfeit truth and limit the good that can be done. This life is a war, a constant fight. If you slap someone in the face, you should expect to be slapped in return at least as hard as you slapped him. We are in a spiritual war, and if the people of God attack the territory of the devil, there will no doubt be a counterattack.

There are a lot of people claiming great outpourings and supernatural signs and wonders. Many of these fill people with a sense of elation for a time, but looking at American Christians today is like looking into the emergency room of a hospital: So many are wounded, lonely, unsuccessful, sick, divorced, addicted, fearful, and unmotivated to get up and make a difference for Jesus in the world. Their idea of honoring God consists of trying to be good and singing with their hands raised at a Sunday morning worship service. Maybe they are "slain in the spirit" from time to time, but their problems still overwhelm them. They receive prophecies of all the great things they will do someday, and they "put them on the shelf" and just continue in the same rut that they can't get out of. Certainly not all Christians live defeated lives. But for all the revivals and outpourings that are supposedly going on all over the country, there are far too many "spirit-filled" Christians who are demonized, unable to overcome their problems, and living lives no different than unbelievers.

True Worship, and Prophecy that Edifies

Worshiping God and seeking His presence, peace, and joy can be an emotional experience—an experience we should all seek. Singing with all of our hearts, raising our hands to Him, and rejoicing in His presence are all a wonderful part of our communion with Him. Churches who stifle this kind of worship are not allowing the Holy Spirit to minister to His people as freely as He would like. Each of us needs to understand how small and helpless we are before His majesty and to speak to Him from our hearts, both at home and in the fellowship of our church. Those who are not yet free from demonic oppression can also be touched by the Holy Spirit and feel His presence; those who are not even saved can feel Him and have their spiritual eyes opened to see Him as the Lord.

In Africa, dancing is a normal part of their culture, and it easily found its way into the worship time of our services. But part of worship is listening to the voice of God in our spirits and meditating on His Word. Music, clapping, prayers, audibly crying out to God, dancing, and silence in His presence all have an important part to play in the church as we reach out to our Father in heaven. But when praise and worship time is considered more important than hearing and obeying God's Word, it can easily become a fleshly experience where feelings and emotions take over.

Prophecies that instruct us in specific concerns and situations not mentioned in the Bible need to come through the intelligence and rational thought of a godly man or woman who has a true experience with God. Pastors who study the Word, pray for their congregations, cry out for the lost souls that need salvation, and seek God for direction will find God's answer through a conviction in their heart as God's Word works in their mind and spirit. When they share their concerns with other men of God and use the Bible as their final authority, God gives them direction to know what choices to make and what steps of faith to take no matter how risky. They receive their "word of knowledge" not from a vision, a hot flash, or getting knocked over on their backs in a trance, but in humility and submission to the appointed leaders of their church and to the greatest prophecy of all—the Bible.

While all pastors must be, in effect, prophets for their congregations, God desires to speak to all of His children. Romans 12:2 tells us, "And do not be conformed to this world, but be transformed by the renewing of your mind, so that you may prove what the will of God is, that which is good and acceptable and perfect." It's as simple as that! As we die to this world in our desires and our actions and as we renew our mind by meditating on God's Word, we will be able to test and approve His will. We don't need signs and wonders to know the desires of our Heavenly Father; it's so clear and straightforward, yet we make it something mysterious and complicated. Christians would rather have God appear with the best Hollywood special effects than to hear Him speak in a still small voice as He did to Elijah.

In all these supernatural manifestations—some of which are even more bizarre than just falling over, such as laughing, roaring, leaping, "Holy Ghost glue," drunkenness, gold fillings, and gold dust—the danger is that when a person is seeking a spiritual experience that is not of God, the devil can enter that person's life to possess them. Since returning to the U.S., I can't count how many people I have counseled who have experienced these manifestations. They are convinced that they are baptized in the Holy Spirit, yet they are suffering so much demonic oppression that it's clear they are possessed. They claim to be gifted with words of knowledge and prophecy, yet they're unemployed, deep in debt, plagued with mystery illnesses and divorced. Their pride blocks them from understanding that those words of knowledge are just a deception, otherwise they would have all the blessings that they needed to overcome. Faith without intelligence is a powerful ploy of the devil. He does not seek to turn us into atheists but to make us weak, ineffective, and pitiful in the eyes of the world. And in some cases, even our salvation can be lost if we lose heart and give up the fight.

In one of his letters to him, Paul encourages Timothy, "Pay close attention to yourself and to your teaching; persevere in these things, for as you do this you will ensure salvation both for yourself and for those who hear you" (1 Timothy 4:16). The doctrines that we believe in affect our lives as well as the lives of all those around us.

CHAPTER TWELVE

Intelligent Faith

When Argentina was a teenager, a chronic pain developed in her right leg. It eventually became swollen and unbearable to walk on. Her mother was a prominent member in the local Methodist Church in Mozambique, but when their pastor told them to accept this sickness as the will of God, they sought help anywhere else they could. After two years of hopeless searching, her father took her on the long and tiresome trip to neighboring Zambia, to live with a witchdoctor and find a cure for her diseased leg. She lived there for a year, taking all the potions and going through all the rituals she could—drinking the blood of goats and chickens and calling upon the spirits of her ancestors—but she got even worse.

Her parents then took her to South Africa and had her admitted to a well-respected hospital in Johannesburg to receive medical treatment. They had to sell all of their household possessions to get the deposit for her admission. After a year of living in the hospital, unable to walk or even sleep at night because of the pain, the doctors decided to risk an operation to unblock a vein in her right leg that was though to be the cause of everything. If unsuccessful, her leg would be amputated because gangrene was beginning to set in. She agreed to the procedure, reasoning that a plastic leg would be a thousand times better than constant pain and being unable to walk or live a normal life.

The day before her surgery was to take place, prayer counselors from the church came to the hospital to pray for the sick. They found Argentina in great pain and very bitter about her life. They prayed for her, rebuking the sickness and any demons that might be in her life. She had no faith that the prayer would work, but to her amazement, that night she slept peacefully for the first time in four years. The next day she was feeling so good from the night's rest that she decided to try and walk to the bathroom—something she hadn't been able to do for years. Moving very slowly and steadying herself on the wall and chairs, she actually made it to the bottom on her own. She was thrilled. Sure that God would help her even more, she waited anxiously for the prayer counselors to return as they had promised. They came and asked the doctor's permission to take her to the church.

She had never seen a church that cast out demons before, and at first she was skeptical and confused. When the prayers began, she manifested violent demons that had been living inside of her for many years. In her manifesting state she walked as if nothing was wrong, even jumping, kicking and fighting with the pastor who was praying for her. When asked, the demons spoke and declared that they were responsible for bringing the disease to her leg.

When the demons were all cast out, she looked around, surprised. Some of the pastors' shirts had been grabbed and ripped and their ties had been twisted, and everyone was sweating and panting—but also smiling, because the power of Jesus Christ had set her free. That day she walked normally for the first time in four years. As days and weeks went by, all the swelling in her leg went down, the surgery was cancelled, and, to the doctors amazement, she was given a clean bill of health.

A week or so after arriving home from the hospital, she began to reason that if God had really healed her she should be able not only to walk but to run. She had noticed a neighbor who jogged every day, and she approached him, asking if he would teach her how to run. He replied that she should join the running club that he was a part of, the Long Distance Running Club of Gauteng. She did, but she was only able to walk in the first week or two of training. However, soon she was running great distances. There was a ten-kilometer race to decide which women would represent the club in professional races; the ten fastest women would be chosen. Argentina, only a few months after leaving the hospital, came in seventh place and became a part of the club's team.

Now Argentina is a professional marathon runner. She is one of the fastest women in the country of South Africa and has been a part of the national team for several years. She has a trove of medals and is improving her times with each race. Her favorite races are ultramarathons that can involve distances of almost a hundred kilometers. She loves to run, and she loves to prove to everyone who knows her that God is real and alive—and that He answers prayer.

The Five Senses

Faith in God contradicts what we consider as intelligence. At least that's what we're taught in school. We're taught to believe in what we can taste, touch, hear, see, and smell—that which can be proven in a lab, what is physically concrete. Faith and human reasoning do conflict with each other most of the time, but it doesn't have to be that way. The five senses are not all that we have to navigate through this life. Think of it this way: Though you can touch and see your red car parked in the driveway, it is not more real or life-changing than the love that keeps a couple married for thirty years. One is easily proven because it can be seen; the other exists but is impossible to physically measure or hold. Even scientists and researchers confess that there are things which haven't yet been discovered or explained. Just because something is not visible to the naked eye doesn't automatically mean that it's not there. Microscopes, telescopes, X-rays, CAT scans, and blood tests all reveal the existence of things we can't normally see. There is much more to our world that we cannot see, but technology hasn't developed far enough to discover these things. Pure logic demands that we must acknowledge there are things that exist which we cannot see right now.

The Bible takes this one step further when it declares, "So we fix our eyes not on what is seen, but on what is unseen. For what is seen is temporary, but what is unseen is eternal" (2 Corinthians 4:18). Here, the Bible reveals that there is another dimension to life, and that this "unseen," invisible part is more real than the "seen"—the complete opposite of the way most people go about their lives in this world.

Though faith is believing in what is unseen, using our intelligence is essential for faith to be effective. Real faith is not blind and ignorant, but intelligent. Argentina's argument—that if she was really healed by God she should be able to become a professional long-distance runner—was based upon an intelligent faith in God. Her conclusion makes sense! She wanted to test her body to see if her healing was really a miracle from God; if it was, she knew she'd be able to run as far and as fast as she wanted. And so, courageously, she began to do something she'd never done before. Intelligent faith is not emotion, hype, or illusion, it's the real thing.

Living Faith

"Now faith is the assurance of things hoped for, the conviction of things not seen" (Hebrews 11:1).

Describing the way a believer should live, the apostle Paul says that "we walk by faith, not by sight" (2 Corinthians 5:7). This doesn't mean that we close our eyes when crossing a busy street, or that we spend our days blindly stumbling through life. Not in the least. It means that faith is our guide. It means that we boldly choose not to make decisions based on what we see but on the conviction of God in our hearts. When Jairus's friends came and told him that his daughter was dead and that he should not bother Jesus any more, Jesus overheard what they said yet chose not to let it influence His behavior. Jesus turned to Jairus and said, "Do not be afraid any longer; only believe, and she will be made well." This great passage gives us insight into the true nature of faith.

Another example, on a very mundane scale, is when you pass your test for a driver's license. In the state of California you are given a temporary license made of a few pieces of photocopied paper stapled together. You can walk out the door, get in your car, and drive away at ease, knowing that the license is already yours. You don't hold it in your hands yet, but you have all the evidence you need to know that it is coming in the mail in a week or so. You can live and act as if it is already in your possession because your temporary license is enough. This, on a very basic level, is faith. If you transfer this concept to the spiritual level, it is much the same. Faith is unseen, but it is far more than an idea: *It is a conviction so solid, so unmovable, that it is as if the answer to your prayers has already been fulfilled.* In chapter one, Evelyn explained how she felt when she began to have real faith that her rare eye disease would be healed. She described it as having "a joy and an assurance in my heart that something wonderful was about to happen. I felt this peace that made no logical sense whatsoever; it just came naturally rather than being forced. As the days went by, the peace in my heart never wavered no matter what happened around me."

This was Hebrews 11:1 coming alive in her heart—the conviction her faith brought was all she needed. She had a profound confirmation deep in her heart that what she was asking for and believing in was actually going to happen. It was a kind of spiritual proof that produced an unshakable, unwavering confidence in her future healing; it didn't matter that it hadn't already happened because she knew that it would happen. Only when a person feels this confirmation can he truly "wait on the Lord," as Scripture encourages countless times, because only when you are sure that an answer is coming can you wait. No one waits for something he doesn't believe is coming. Faith is the ability to trust that God is in control and that He will answer you because you are His child.

To those who don't know God or who have never known this unwavering confidence that doesn't depend on anything physical, faith is considered foolish and fanatical, a pitiful delusion. They may even suggest that a person who lives by faith is living in denial, afraid to face the facts. Faith is seen as a crutch, a weakness. But for those who know Him and have experienced His presence and power, these statements couldn't be farther from the truth. Paul explains it this way:

*"... and my message and my preaching were not in persua-
sive words of wisdom, but in demonstration of the Spirit and
of power, so that your faith would not rest on the wisdom of
men, but on the power of God... But a natural man does
not accept the things of the Spirit of God, for they are foolishness to him; and he cannot understand them, because
they are spiritually appraised"* (1 Corinthians 2:4,5,14).

Can Faith and Intelligence Coexist?

Take a closer look at the subject of faith. It's not as simple as it looks. There are a host of men and women who conquered by faith, who were able to do impossible things through the power of God. They were intelligent men and women who were able to overpower enemies and transform cities and nations into great successes. No one denies the fact that King David was the greatest king of Israel and that through his leadership the country gained the respect of the known world. He was a man of faith, yet to rule the country and develop the nation of Israel as he did, he had to be a man of intelligence also. Faith and intelligence don't have to be in conflict.

The intelligence of a person of faith is an intelligence based on humility. It acknowledges the existence and greatness of God. It acknowledges that only He can bring true fulfillment and that each one of us are wretched and worthless sinners in comparison. It recognizes that man cannot and should not depend on himself alone. When we believe that we are self-sufficient as human beings, that we don't need anyone, that we can accomplish all things through knowledge, science, and learning, we are basically asserting that we are gods. This is the philosophy of humanism that dominates our entire society today. Man thinks he is the center of the universe. In this we commit the worst possible sin: to assume that we don't need God. It's full-blown pride at its worst, the kind of pride that blinds us to the truth. Intelligent faith, on the other hand, is fully aware of our desperate need for God.

Marriage is a good example of how dependency on others can be healthy and strengthening. Evelyn and I have been through some tough times in our twenty years of marriage—her blindness, the beginning of our ministry in New York City, nine years in Africa, a near-death experience with our youngest son, Mark, and all the normal difficulties of marriage. After these many years, I can't go through a day without talking to her. When I'm away from her on a trip (which I try to avoid), I don't feel like my normal self, and I can't wait to see her again.

Am I weak because I need my wife? Am I weaker now than when I was single? No. I feel an overwhelming need to be close to her because I love her and because I realize she has helped me develop into a better man. Things that she sees and feels and understands as a woman have taught me that there is another side to life. And by developing my abilities and learning from her, I have become a stronger, more well-rounded man. It would be sheer foolishness for me not to acknowledge these facts. The communication, the friendship, the love, and the support are all things that I don't want to be without any more. I need her not because I'm weak, but because she has added to my life and taken me to heights that I couldn't reach without her.

We live by faith because our intellect instructs us that we can accomplish much more when we are allied with God. He is our Creator, the one who knows us best. He loves us with a love we will never be able to comprehend. It makes perfect sense for us to run to Him, to long to be close to Him every moment of our lives. In fact, it's ridiculous to even consider living our life out of communion with Him.

Intelligence demands that we acknowledge the physical properties and limitations of this world and make use of them the best we can. We can't float along on some other-worldly plane and ignore the responsibilities of ordinary life like some guru or mystic. We live by faith, but we still have to deal with the mundane—get a job, pay our bills, take the kids to school, etc. Yet our intelligence doesn't stop at the empirical; it goes beyond the limits of our five senses to include the promises of God.

Intelligent Faith Requires Strength of Character

"Jesus promised 'A' if I do 'B.' So I will do 'B,' just as He said, and I *know* 'A' will happen." It sounds like a very childish way of life, but take a look at what these great promises are:

- Love your enemies; do good to them; lend to them and don't expect anything back. Your reward will be great; you will be a son of the Most High (see Luke 6:35).
- Do not judge, you will not be judged; forgive and you will be forgiven; give and it will be given to you; a good measure, pressed down, shaken together, and running over, will be poured into your lap (see Luke 6:37-38).
- If any one wants to be first, he must be the very last, and the servant of all (see Mark 9:35).
- Bless those who persecute you; do not repay anyone evil with evil; do not take revenge, but leave room for God's wrath; overcome evil with good (see Romans 12:17-21).
- Submit yourselves to God; resist the devil and he will flee from you; humble yourselves before the Lord, and He will lift you up (see James 4:7-10).
- Is anyone sick? Call the elders to pray and anoint him with oil and the sick will be made well (see James 5:14).
- If you have faith as small as a mustard seed; tell a mountain to move from here to there and it will move; nothing will be impossible for you (see Matthew 17:20).
- Whatever you ask for in prayer, believe that you have received it, and it will be yours (see Mark 11:24).
- Consider it pure joy when you face trials of many kinds; you will become mature and complete, not lacking anything (see James 1:2).
- Delight yourself in the Lord and He will give you the desires of your heart (see Psalms 37:4).

These commands and promises sound like nonsensical, foolish ideas to the ordinary man of the world. But to truly believe and have the courage to daily walk in these commands requires strength of character and discipline of the mind, body, and spirit. Rather than becoming a mindless, blind follower, a person who lives by faith carefully chooses his actions and thoughts based on God's commands. Thus, he becomes even more alive, aware, and empowered to do far more than anyone else around him.

Faith with intelligence sees beyond the ordinary limits of our world and knows that even the laws of nature can be changed when faith is put into action. But God has given us our own set of instructions and limitations that we cannot break, even though we may think we have a great faith. This is what makes faith something solid and sure—not magical or mystical as many imagine it to be. For example, He promises us that if we have the faith of a mustard seed, we can do the impossible. But He also says that He is against those who are proud. So perhaps we find a man of great zeal performing miracles, but eventually we see him fall into disgrace or lose his reputation as a man of God. This is because the promises of God are true. He had faith to see his prayers answered, but his heart was corrupt and full of pride, so God had to discipline him by bringing him down.

It is essential for those who desire to live by faith to know and understand the Word of God fully. If we emphasize one aspect of His promises and ignore another, we are not exercising an intelligent faith but a form of religiosity. That's how we end up with cults, fanatical believers who emphasize works or the gifts of the Spirit over humility, politically driven churches that interpret the Bible purely for the sake of social action, and just your ordinary church that tries its best to do the work of God but has little or no effect in changing people's lives.

"That Was Then, This Is Now"

It's this last type of church—the one that tries to do the work of God but has little effect in changing people's lives—that I believe is most typical of the churches in the United States. They never get into the news or have famous pastors running for office. They are not known for great outpourings or signs and wonders. They are teaching the Bible, but their overriding theme is that God cares mostly about our moral behavior and how we treat those around us. All miracles and works of power are relegated to the "that was then, this is now" category. Meanwhile the members of the church are sadly watching their children rejecting God for the more exciting life of the world; they are holding the hands of their dying spouses who have succumbed to incurable diseases; they are struggling through each day to make ends meet; they are enduring the ridicule of co-workers who have no love for God.

On one hand, God is pleased to see them trying to keep their spirits up, showing love and patience during difficult times, and faithfully attending church despite the fact that the only reward they can feel sure of is life after death. On the other hand, do you think God is pleased to see that His children don't take His Word seriously when he commands them to pray for the sick? Or when He instructs them to fight the devil, destroy strongholds, and live a life of victory? It's as if they don't really believe He answers prayer or that He loves them enough to rescue them from trouble.

To human eyes, these believers can appear to be wonderful Christians, but the fact remains that they are not truly believing in God and using His power to overcome and be a light for Him in this dark world. They have the authority of God to wrestle lives out of the hands of Satan, but instead they choose to watch them slip away while silently asking God, "Why?" They are unbalanced Christians who discourage others from following Christ because of their weak testimony. Their faith is sweet and kind, but ineffective.

Romans 12:2 says, "Do not conform any longer to the pattern of this world, but be transformed by the renewing of your mind. Then you will be able to test and approve what God's will is—His good, pleasing and perfect will." It's interesting that the Holy Spirit teaches us to renew our minds, not just our behavior or even our hearts. We are expected by God to use our intellect—not merely as the world does but as He does. Renewing our minds can only be done when His Word becomes the most important source of information in our life. When we know who He is—His character, His power, and His desires for us—even the smallest details of our lives become clear and understandable. We know that He promised to give us life in abundance, but we are suffering want; logic tells us we should discover what is wrong and what is keeping the promises from coming true. Are we being lazy or proud? Living in sin, doubt, fear? Harboring unforgiveness or grudges? All of these things play a big part in whether or not a prayer is effective.

But a pat explanation or a troubleshooting guide to knowing God's will and getting what you want is not the answer. It is the renewing of your mind, which creates a relationship with your Lord Jesus Christ. You come to know Him intimately, feel His presence, love what He loves, and hate what He hates. When a problem arises, you can feel the anger that your Lord feels against the demonic forces that are trying to harm you or someone you love. You know instantaneously that though He has allowed you to go through that problem to purify your faith, He fully intends for you to attack it with your prayers and to trust that He will be faithful according to His Word. And through all the prayers and changes in your life that you know God wants you to make, you have the deep conviction that God will be faithful and answer you in His perfect time. As Paul told Timothy in his second letter, "...because I know whom I have believed, and am convinced that He is able to guard what I have entrusted to Him for that day." Paul was able to endure all the persecution and hardships that came with being a minister of the Gospel because he knew who he believed in—he really *knew* who his Lord was.

CHAPTER THIRTEEN

Abraham's Reasoning

Oscar's Story

I arrived at the clinic at five o'clock that cold, rainy morning in Cape Town, South Africa. I knew the clinic wouldn't open until eight, but I was so sure about my healing that I couldn't sleep at all the night before and decided to get there before anyone else so that I could be the first to be tested. I didn't care that I had to wait for three hours.

When the doors opened we all went into the large waiting room and sat down. As was usual for a Monday morning, there were a lot of people waiting. After an hour the nurse at the reception desk called out my name over the PA system, "Oscar, what are you here for?" The room was big and I was clear on the other side. She asked me again, "What did you come to do?"

I stood up and answered back loudly, "I came for an HIV test."

I knew I had been healed after the Sunday morning prayer in the church. I had felt the power of God so intensely that I was convinced of my healing. But I didn't imagine that I would have to shout about it in front of a crowd of people to see if I really was healed or not! When she asked me the next question, people turned and stared.

"What did you come to do? You were tested three months ago and were found positive. Why are you here to do it again?"

She was not patient enough to wait until I reached her desk, and I had to speak loudly for her to hear, "I came to test again because, in the name of the Lord Jesus Christ, I believe I am free and HIV negative now."

Now everyone looked at me! It was embarrassing, but I thought, *You can talk about me and stare at me, that's not my business. I'm here to confirm my healing and go home with my victory.*

After a long and difficult discussion with the nurses and doctors, who couldn't understand why I wanted to be tested again, I was finally allowed to have my blood taken. The last thing the nurse at reception said to me was, "Go get the test and let's see what your Jesus is going to do for you."

When I came out to wait for the results, the whole waiting room was looking at me. I felt the pressure to prove to everyone that God really did miracles. At that moment I changed the way I was praying and said, *My Jesus, here I am in front of all these people saying that You healed me. If I go home HIV positive they'll never believe in You. Please do this miracle in my life today. Glorify Your name because it's in Your name that I'm here believing that I'm healed. If the results are positive again, the doctors and nurses will never believe that You have the power to do great things.*

Today it's easy to speak about, but at the time it wasn't easy! It was terrible.

After thirty minutes they called me for the results and the nurse seemed to be upset. She said, "Come here! The results are negative. We don't understand. You have to go back and be tested again."

I was happy when she said I was negative, but the way she was acting confused me. It was as if she didn't want me to be negative.

So they took more blood, tested it, and the results were negative again! They called me and all the doctors, nurses, and staff together and showed me the results. They all looked at me and said, "We don't understand. Here are the positive results from three months ago, and here are the negative ones from today. And from your file we see that you've been living with a woman for the last year that tested positive three years ago. We know that you are positive, but the tests don't show it."

Then I said, "I told you I was healed in the name of the Lord Jesus Christ. I'm healed! You can test me as much as you want, but the results will always be negative in the name of Jesus!"

I don't know if I'll ever feel that happiness again! I walked back through the waiting room with a great big smile on my face giving everyone a "thumbs up" with both hands.

Two weeks later they took Oscar up on his offer and asked him to come in again for another test at a different clinic with a different lab. That test came back HIV negative, too.

The woman with whom Oscar had been living had been HIV positive for more than three years, but only after living with Oscar for nine months did she have the courage to tell him the truth about her infection. His first reaction was, "I should kill you and then myself. What's the point in continuing to live?" But after coming to the church and finding Jesus he learned to have a faith that was not only words or feelings but action. He knew that if God was who He said He was, He was able to do the miracle of cleansing his HIV-infected blood.

Oscar had to use his logic and reason. Even though Oscar knew he was healed, God required him to overcome one more fight in order to see the fulfillment of his miracle. For Oscar, to come to church, humble himself before God, and be willing to give up his old, sinful lifestyle, he had to fight against the devil every step of the way. He originally had no hope to ever be healed of this incurable disease and reasoned that if he had to die, he at least wanted to be saved. When the pastor preached about Jesus' miracles and the impossible becoming possible, Oscar reasoned that if God had done such wonderful things in the past, He could still do them today. When the pastor called forward for a special prayer all those who were suffering from incurable diseases, he was the first to jump up and run forward, expecting the Word of God to come true in his life.

But though he was convinced of his healing, he reasoned that, if it were true, he would find proof in the same clinic that had tested him with the disease months before—and he was determined to see the proof with his own eyes. As the devil tried to fight against his faith through the rudeness and unbelief of all the nurses and doctors, Oscar reasoned that the proof of his healing should not be just for his own benefit, but to glorify God right there before all the people in that clinic. He reasoned that it was worth enduring shame, hours of waiting, and bad treatment to honor God that day. And because of his perseverance and determination to see God's Word come true in his life, God honored him greatly. He is now completely healed, blessed, and full of joy. Oscar had an intelligent faith that persevered until he saw his miracle.

This is faith that brings results. The book of James says that faith without works is dead, and this still holds true for any miracle we need. God requires of us to have more than just a warm fuzzy feeling inside that we have received our answer; we must be so convinced and so sure of His blessing that we are willing to act on it, never wavering or doubting. As a part of our fight to overcome, He expects us to reason, think, and use our logic based on the promises in His Word. Those who think that faith means turning off our minds and becoming ignorant have no idea what true faith is.

Abraham's Intelligent Faith

Have you ever asked yourself why God commanded Abraham to sacrifice Isaac on Mount Moriah, a three-day journey from where he was at that time? Why didn't He have him sacrifice Isaac immediately, right there on the spot? I believe that God wanted Abraham's decision to be an intelligent one.

Though Abraham's faith was being challenged like no other time in his life, God did not want him to sacrifice his son out of an emotional reaction. God's voice commanding him to do such a horrific and shocking thing could have sent Abraham into a whirl of emotion. It might have been easier for Abraham to just grab his son and sacrifice him right then and there—while his veins were still pumping with adrenaline in the sheer intensity of the moment—but God did not want Abraham to sacrifice Isaac in a frenzied moment of passion. Rather, He sent him off to bed, letting him think and wonder. Then, the next morning, He led Abraham on a long and tiresome walk, loaded down with a donkey, wood, and two servants. Abraham had to walk side by side with the young son he loved so dearly and for whom he had longed for many years—and whom he now had to sacrifice.

Abraham was forced to think about his decision to obey God—every single moment, every step of the way. He had to think of the implications: What will life be like without Isaac? What will Sarah say? Who will be my descendants? How will I tell Isaac I'm going to kill him? How can I do such a terrible thing? If Abraham was anything like we are today, I'm sure there were times he was tempted to wonder if it really was God who had spoken to him that day. Maybe he wondered if he had misunderstood what God had said, that maybe the part about sacrificing his son was some mistake.

In Hebrews we gain a small insight into Abraham's thoughts on that three-day journey to Moriah. It says:

"By faith Abraham, when he was tested, offered up Isaac, and he who had received the promises was offering up his only begotten son; it was he to whom it was said, 'In Isaac your descendants shall be called.' He considered that God is able to raise people even from the dead, from which he also received him back as a type" (Hebrews 11:17-19).

Abraham didn't have a blind, ignorant faith. The scripture says that during the three-day trip to Mount Moriah he "considered that

God is able." He was thinking. He was using his intelligence. His reasoning took into account the existence of God and His mighty power, and as a result, Abraham had the courage to do what was unthinkable for this physical world—because he knew who God was. He looked at his dilemma through God's eyes, understanding that God was capable of raising the dead. He was also sure that God's promise of making him a great nation through Isaac was something unchangeable. Because of his intelligent and well-thought-out faith, he was inspired to act in a radical but pleasing way before God.

Thousands of years later, God the Father did the very same thing that Abraham had been asked to do: He sacrificed His only begotten Son. By being willing to sacrifice Isaac and by considering that God was able to raise people from the dead, Abraham was taking on the mind and character of God the Father!

An intelligent faith is what made sense of sacrificing Isaac. Abraham knew that beyond all the love he had for his son, his love and obedience to God had to come first. He knew the rewards would be great and that it would be the ultimate proof that he believed. And it really was. As he was about to kill Isaac an angel stopped him and God said, "…for now I know that you fear God, since you have not withheld your son, your only son, from Me" (Genesis 22:12).

> *"For you are all sons of God through faith in Christ Jesus.*
> *For all of you who were baptized into Christ have clothed*
> *yourselves with Christ. There is neither Jew nor Greek, there*
> *is neither slave nor free man, there is neither male nor*
> *female; for you are all one in Christ Jesus. And if you belong*
> *to Christ, then you are Abraham's descendants, heirs accord-*
> *ing to promise"* (Galatians 3:26-29).

We become God's sons and daughters when we have faith. We clothe ourselves with Christ so that, wherever we go, Christ is seen through us. When we truly live by faith, we act as He would, we cause demons to tremble as He would, we silence storms and rebuke diseases as He would. We become Abraham's seed, his descendants—not physical descendants as the Jews are today, but spiritual ones. When we take on the same kind of intelligent faith, based on a personal and loving relationship with our Lord, and we live in a radical way that makes no sense to the world but is in obedience to God's Word, we become just as blessed as Abraham. We inherit the promise God made to him to establish a great nation. We too are able, through this faith, to establish great things to glorify Him.

Quality Faith

It is a given that Christians are people of faith. But faith is a very loosely used term. Faith has come to stand for a creed or religion a kind of cultural tradition that you grow up in, with festivals and rituals that bring families and communities together. You can hear it talked about in the news: "Civil war rages on in such-and-such-land between the two dominant faiths." The Bible, however, never uses the word "faith" with this meaning. In fact, it gives us a description of just two kinds of faith: living and dead. Either you've got it, or you don't!

Of course, if you ask a professing Christian if he has faith, the automatic answer would be yes. Perhaps because he acknowledges all that is stated in the Apostles' Creed he assumes that he is going to heaven. Maybe he is and maybe he's not, but to merely agree with a statement of faith is not faith at all. "Now faith is the assurance of things hoped for, the conviction of things not seen." It is *assurance* and *conviction*. Faith is something that brings what does not exist into existence. It brings peace where there is chaos, love where there is hatred, health where there is sickness, life where there is death.

Jesus told us that we know a tree by its fruit; in the same way, we know a man by the fruit he bears. If he is a man of God, a man of true faith, the fruit of his life will be evident. He will have a life full of victories. Even when problems arise and seem to overcome him for a moment, his faith will rise up even higher and bring about answers to his prayers. But the one who just claims to have faith is helpless in the face of problems. When he is under pressure, it's all he can do to just stay alive, much less overcome.

"Even so faith, if it has no works, is dead, being by itself...
You believe that God is one. You do well; the demons also

believe, and shudder. But are you willing to recognize, you
foolish fellow, that faith without works is useless?... For just
as the body without the spirit is dead, so also faith without
works is dead" (James 2:17,19,20,26).

Since the verses that precede this passage talk about feeding and clothing the poor, most people interpret this scripture to mean social action. God loves and cares about the poor and needy, and there are many references that teach how God wants His children to do the same. Feeding the hungry and being involved in charitable activities are definitely important parts of our lives as Christians because we need to have a heart of compassion as our Lord also has. But these verses are talking about something deeper than just social outreaches.

Faith without action is just an idea, but faith with action is a supernatural force. Finding clothes for a beggar is a simple, physical task. But what about the compassion we need to have for a co-worker who is bound up with evil spirits, who is being destroyed by alcohol or drugs? If all we give them is words, what kind of faith do we have? Telling someone you are there for them and that God loves them could make them feel a small amount of comfort for a time, but what they need is *power*. To bring real results they need strong prayers of deliverance against demons. They need a friend to level with them and help them to see that Jesus still does miracles today. They need a church that can teach them how to fight against their problems.

Faith works with action: laying our hands on someone who is sick and determining their healing in Jesus' name; anointing and praying over the desk of an unbelieving friend at work who is going through depression; finally having the courage to speak out and rebuke your rebellious teenagers, knowing that God has given you the authority to bless and protect them. True faith demands that we act on it. If we expect faith to work based on a sensation of peace we felt during a prayer but refuse to act in a way that proves we believe, we will be useless. Faith is a fight against the thoughts of the devil that bring doubts and worry. It is a determination to act as if the answer is already yours. Faith cannot work without boldness and a willingness to look like a fool in the eyes of everyone else. Without action, faith is dead.

Prayers that Really Work

Just as the word "faith" has lost its true meaning in this world, so has the idea of prayer. It's sickening to listen to politicians addressing some terrible tragedy saying, "The victims and their families are in our prayers." What in the world does that mean? It's just a neat sound bite. It makes Mr. Politics look compassionate and spiritual, and it gives a vague suggestion that he's actually doing something about the problem.

Prayer has also been reduced to a last resort effort. There have been times when I've told people that I would be praying for them—that I would really pray in true faith, that God was giving me the conviction that He would resolve their problem. But they would just smile at me in a surprised and kind of pitying way, shake their head, and thank me for my quaint and old-fashioned courtesy. What a slap in God's face! Prayer that is made in true and intelligent faith is power! It is the connection we have with our almighty, omnipotent Lord, and to treat it as anything less is an act of the greatest disrespect to God.

Isn't this what we see today, even among Christians? Some people pray and see great blessings. Others pray and see nothing out of the ordinary. Abraham did not have the same life as Lot, even though they had the same opportunities, lived in the same place, and had the same God. One had quality faith that caused him to act in an extraordinary way; the other had a faith that did not work at all. When five kings attacked Sodom and Gomorrah and took Lot and four other kings captive, Abraham rounded up 318 men born in his household, destroyed those five kings, and released Lot and the other four kings. Abraham, with a small band of men, did what four kings and their armies could not!

Abraham lived in prosperity and blessing even when he allowed Lot to choose the best land to live in and Abraham was only left with the desert. Lot ended up in Sodom and Gomorrah and lost everything he had, including his wife. Abraham could do what Lot could not do, simply because his faith was living and Lot's was not.

Real faith and effective prayers only come from radical people—people who are ready to face death for the sake of Christ, people who have no fear to rush into a battle against demons. A special friend and fellow pastor was a great example to me. Whenever he heard bad news, he would laugh and rub his hands together and say, "Do you see? The devil is angry, I must be doing something right!" His attitude was that every attack of the devil was a challenge to fight back with the power of God and see another victory. He reasoned that if God gave us the authority to bind up the devil and overcome all our enemies, we have no reason at all to worry or be afraid.

Prayers that work are based on the fact that we have authority in the name of Jesus Christ. No one with living faith who really knows how to pray can live a normal life. His vision of the world is different. He has recovered the position that Adam lost in the garden when God said, "Let Us make man in Our image, according to Our likeness; and let them rule over the fish of the sea and over the birds of the sky and over the cattle and over all the earth" (Genesis 1:26). What Adam lost through his obedience to the voice of the devil, we regain through a life of faith, a life of communion with God, a life of dependence on Him. That is when we take on the nature and characteristics of God. We begin to think like He thinks, see like He sees, and act like He acts. When we use God's authority to conquer the problems and limitations around us, we can truly say that the devil is defeated.

Prayer is our connection with God, and it can cause us to feel great strength, joy, peace, and determination. But *effective* prayer begins from an intelligent faith that expects the Word of God to come true today, in our lives, right now. If I am absolutely sure that God has given me authority over all the demons that are attacking me, I can pray with all my heart for God to destroy the evil around me, demand the demons to be tied up and cast out, call down the power of God to take control of the situation, and accomplish His will. When I am finished, I can rest and be completely at peace because I know He has heard me and is answering me even before I see the miracle. This may sound too extreme, too simplistic. But this is exactly the way that God expects His children to act—with simple faith!

Some people argue that faith is a gift, that we can't expect everyone to believe in great things, that some are chosen for that purpose and others are chosen to live more mundane lives. God didn't create us for mundane lives! The Bible says that faith is a gift, but we are all chosen to be overcomers. We are all commanded to live by faith. Faith is something supernatural, something that we cannot fabricate by ourselves by speaking a certain way, jumping around, or acting enthusiastic about a prayer we want answered. It comes from the Spirit of God working within us.

But faith doesn't just drop out of the sky. We don't just wake up one morning and find out that we have it. Faith is a gift that must be sought after and used for the glory of God. Perhaps we are all born with the gift of faith lying dormant within us, waiting to be awakened. Or perhaps it is a gift given only to those who seek it. Either way, we can't accept a life without it or make excuses for why we don't have it. We are expected by God to have a living and active faith, full of results that change our world. That's what He created us for.

"For we are His workmanship, created in Christ Jesus for good works, which God prepared beforehand so that we would walk in them" (Ephesians 2:10).

CHAPTER FOURTEEN

Good Fruit...Good Tree

"Blessed is the man who trusts in the Lord and whose trust is in the Lord. 'For he will be like a tree planted by the water, that extends its roots by a stream and will not fear when heat comes; but its leaves will be green, and it will not be anxious in a year of drought nor cease to yield fruit" (Jeremiah 17:7-8).

This verse is supposed to be about us. This beautiful verse is a promise of abundance in every area of our lives, no matter what the situation is around us. Its not just talking about finances, but fruitfulness in all things: health, joy, wisdom, abilities, strength, and much more. The man who trusts in the Lord has no fear of heat or drought; he goes on growing and producing fruit despite all odds. He is free of anxiety—not just because everything is working out for him, but because he knows that it is his Father's will for him to be fruitful at all times and because he knows that he can use his faith to overcome any problem.

Being truly free from the oppression of the devil requires far more than making a prayer to accept Jesus into our lives or getting rid of bad habits or even becoming a moral and "good" person. Finding salvation is the most important of all, of course, but it is just the beginning. Salvation is a daily process and a daily fight. The Bible says that we should work out our salvation with fear and trembling (see Philippians 2:12), because He is the one at work in us, and we are to work for His good pleasure. God's good pleasure is far more pleasurable and beautiful than any pleasure we could imagine. His handiwork is good and right and perfect. A true and free believer understands that he, as a sinner, is both worthless and evil and, at the same time, precious and made holy because of God's wonderful grace.

No Christian doubts that Jeremiah 17:7,8 is a wonderful passage. But many who are going through drought and scorching heat see it merely as words of comfort to help the suffering endure. But that is not what the promise says. It doesn't say, "Blessed is the man who hangs on and endures. Somehow he'll survive if he's lucky. And, if he doesn't, well, God moves in mysterious ways." God fully intends for us to expect this kind of fruitful life. If it's not happening, we need to do whatever it takes to learn how to have this enduring trust that brings about God's promised results. The Bible is meant to be taken literally.

Those who believe in creation over evolution are emphatic about the literal interpretation of the Bible, and I wholeheartedly agree. But when it comes to seeing answers to our needs and to our prayers their arguments become fuzzy, and they are full of excuses as to why the Bible is not coming true in their lives. They may argue that "that was then, this is now" or that the promises were merely poetic exaggerations of how God really works.

Every true Christian is given the power and authority necessary to overcome in every area of his life. And when he fails, God's love and mercy is so great that He gives the sinner another chance to overcome again. It is God's desire for you to be exactly like the fruitful tree. If these verses in Jeremiah don't typify your life, you may not know what it means to really trust in God. Maybe you're not listening to the convictions or counsel of the Holy Spirit, maybe you really don't know God at all. But either way, very few Christians wrestle in their prayers and in their spiritual life to make sure this promise comes true for them.

Filling Your House with the Holy Spirit

When Jesus told us that demons cannot return to a house that is occupied, He meant that we are only safe from demonic possession when we turn over the ownership of our lives to Him. Being completely free and staying free begins with salvation, but our spiritual freedom can only be guaranteed as we work out that salvation, live by faith each day, and expect to see great things in our lives according to God's will.

The baptism of the Holy Spirit is incredibly important because that is when we willfully allow Him to indwell us and take control of our lives. Demons try to possess us without our knowledge or consent, but the Holy Spirit only takes ownership of our lives when we earnestly seek Him. The Holy Spirit is at work all over the world, drawing people to God, giving wisdom to those who pray, comforting those who mourn, and stimulating those whose hearts are open to receive salvation. Those who make their first steps to being saved are being transformed by the work of the Holy Spirit; it is His work of regeneration that brings about their salvation. But they are not yet baptized in the Holy Spirit.

When the twelve disciples walked with Jesus, cast out demons, and healed the sick, they were not yet baptized in the Holy Spirit but they were saved (excluding Judas who Jesus called a devil). But when the Holy Spirit came upon them, they were transformed men. The changes in their lives began when they first dedicated their lives to serving and obeying Jesus, but the most dramatic transformation came when they were baptized in the Holy Spirit. Crude and uneducated fishermen were able to boldly stand before crowds and give powerful and eloquent messages that pierced the people's hearts. Peter preached to a crowd at Jerusalem and three thousand were saved that very day. The cowardly and bumbling bunch of disciples, whom Jesus had patiently taught for three years, were turned into courageous warriors of faith by their baptism in the Holy Spirit. The same guys who couldn't stay awake to pray with Jesus in the Garden of Gethsemane and who deserted Him at His death considered it an honor to be tortured and even to die for their Lord—all because of their transformed lives after the day of Pentecost.

The baptism in the Holy Spirit is not just the ability to speak in strange tongues; it is the ability to live in God's power in this evil world and to never be overcome. The proof of this baptism is in the fruit that we bear.

> *"But the fruit of the Spirit is love, joy, peace, patience, kindness, goodness, faithfulness, gentleness, self-control; against such things there is no law. Now those who belong to Christ Jesus have crucified the flesh with its passions and desires"* (Galatians 5:22-26).

When our character falls in line with Christ's character, when we bear each and every one of these fruit in our lives no matter what is going on around us or how terrible our persecution, we can be sure that we are baptized in the Holy Spirit. That is when we are able to speak in tongues—true tongues that come from heaven—and to hear His words of guidance and direction clearly. It is a supernatural baptism that comes from God, but it only comes to those who seek it and sacrifice their own desires to live according to His.

It's impossible for our flesh to feel peace in the middle of horrible situations; this peace that comes from the Holy Spirit cannot be faked or created by our own force of will. But even though it is a gift, we have to do our part to receive it. We must try our best to live in His peace. The same goes for all the other fruit of the Spirit, which we can demonstrate from time to time when the circumstances are right, but the true fruit of the Holy Spirit dominates our lives even when it makes no sense to our flesh. Receiving the baptism of the Holy Spirit requires our effort and faith, but, at the same time, it is a power that is far beyond our understanding and natural abilities.

Through this baptism, power can flow through us to perform healings, deliverance, and all sorts of miracles and the gifts of the

Spirit, as mentioned in 1 Corinthians 12, can be manifest in our lives. Because we have Christ's character, we can have the real faith that we need to see the impossible happen in our lives, and we are able to show Him to others through our testimonies. With His Spirit working and leading us each day, it becomes easy to spot the attacks and false accusations of the devil, and by His power we can easily fight back and see our victory.

Because a Christian is not succeeding in his life does not automatically mean that he is demonized. Failures, mistakes, and struggles are all a part of growing and maturing in our faith. But *constant* failure and *unending* cycles of blocked ways and disappointments are sure signs that Satan has free reign in a Christian's life, and that poor suffering believer needs to have those demons cast out before he'll be able to see any kind of change. In much the same way, a Christian who is baptized in the Holy Spirit doesn't automatically become perfect and sinless—unfortunately! But the presence of the Holy Spirit filling and leading him gives him power and strength to overcome the most impossible problems and to know God in a deep, profound way.

Does God Discriminate?

As I said before, the final authority and foundation for our lives has to be the Word of God. If what I believe or teach is fundamentally unbiblical, then it is false. Of course, different schools of thought have debated over specific points in the Bible. These debates have raged on and on (or maybe I should say "droned on," depending on your point of view). Clearly there are some absolute and unchangeable doctrines that no true Christian can debate. But God also reveals Himself to us in our experiences and through our daily relationship with Him. When we see His power and answers to prayer in our lives, we really get to know Him as a Father and a friend. God wants us to have more than just knowledge about Him; He wants us to experience Him.

Ever since I began working in Africa, I have been convinced that God is an abundantly good and loving God. The miracles I saw in that continent amazed me—and humbled me to realize that I had been such an uptight, doubting Christian until then. Even after seeing the healing of my wife's eyes, I didn't understand just how vast God's power was or how much He longs to answer any of us who cry out to Him for a miracle. Of course, even now I don't understand His greatness as I should. But after seeing some of the poorest, most forgotten, and rejected people receive miraculous healings, jobs, families, and the joy of salvation in the Lord Jesus, my vision for what God wants to do in each of our lives just exploded. I thought I was going to lead the lost to Jesus in Africa, but their pure and simple faith led me to experience Him in a life-changing way.

In Africa, I saw the deaf hear, the mute speak and the blind see. I saw AIDS victims healed (both adults and infants), the crippled walk, and the demon possessed set free. I saw murderers, thieves, and rapists truly converted and living transformed lives in Jesus. I saw abusive husbands repent and recreate their homes into loving and happy families. I saw witchdoctors saved, baptized in the Holy Spirit, and training to become pastors and church volunteers. I have seen the stories of the Bible become a reality before my eyes, week after week. If God is so good and loving to the people of Africa, do you think it's because He loves them more than the countless weak and defeated American Christians who are praying and praying but getting no answer? Is God a racial profiler?

I know it's a ridiculous question, but there is definitely a difference between the faith and expectations of the Africans with whom I have worked and what I see among American believers. I'm not pretending that every single African that came into the church saw the answer to all his prayers or that none who we brought to salvation ever fell away. The devil still worked hard to bring doubts and confusion to everyone we ministered to, and there definitely were problems and disappointments that we couldn't ignore. But in general, I found a faith among the people in Africa that deeply affected my own faith. It was a determined, relentless faith, sure that God would be faithful to honor His promises. The real difference I saw between the faith of the Africans and that of the Americans is the simplicity—the childlike quality that touches the heart of God.

I am sure there are plenty of American readers who will take exception to the statements I have made about weak Christians in this country, but it's time to be honest and see that God can do much more through us than what we have seen. After experiencing the incredible love of God for His children on the African continent, I am determined that He wants to demonstrate that same love to us here, if we would just be humble and admit that we don't know Him as we should. The devil has been having a field day—deceiving and confusing us and inflating the egos of our Christian leaders—and God is waiting for us to get back to the basics of what it means to really belong to Him.

What Shall We Then Do?

God has provided all the weapons we need to overcome in this world, as well as all the love and strength to use them properly. It is pointless for us to question why God doesn't do more to change this rotten world. His desire is to use each one of us to change the world. He has chosen us to be his "partners" in revealing His goodness and glory to this world. This partnership requires such a small amount of effort on our part; He has already accomplished His part by sending His Son to die for us on the cross, defeating the devil and setting us free from his power. All we have to do is receive Him into our hearts as our Lord and Savior, reject all evil, live by faith, be transformed by His Spirit, and fight the good fight until the end. It is simple, but it is not an easy thing to do.

Demon-possessed believers can become very complicated people because they have so much confusion and contradictions in their lives. The following list outlines steps to clear up this confusion and find true freedom in Christ. How do we take all these questions and doubts and layers of disappointment and fear and reduce our focus to these simple steps? Only with humility and perseverance.

- Be brutally honest with yourself and recognize that knowledge and church experience have not brought you to the place where God wants you.
- Be humble and forget all your spiritual "credentials"—no one has credentials before God.
- Stop questioning why God has allowed all these problems to plague you, and pay more attention to what you can do to

overcome them. You'll understand all the "whys" later as God reveals them to you.

- Give absolute ownership of your life to Christ so that He can eventually fill you with His Holy Spirit.
- Stop speaking in tongues and getting involved in prophecies and dreams. By eliminating these for the time being you are blocking the devil's chances to deceive you more.
- Submit and be faithful to a church that knows how to cast out demons and how to teach and encourage you in your process of deliverance—don't just to go through a "deliverance session" in a ministry, especially one that charges a fee.
- Be baptized again in water to determine that you are truly going to put to death your flesh.
- Fight against the demons that have been tormenting you—by fighting against sin, fear, doubts, grudges, and all other forms of evil that have been at work in your life.
- Earnestly seek the presence of God and His wisdom each day of your life.
- Begin to pray for the baptism in the Holy Spirit, and live as best you can to bear the fruit of the Holy Spirit by your own strength until the time comes that He baptizes you and empowers you to live on a new spiritual level.
- Find joy in fighting the devil and overcoming his attacks every day.
- Spread the Good News of Jesus' power through your testimony and develop a desire to save souls above all things.
- Live for Jesus and be willing to suffer, sacrifice, and even die for His name's sake—for you are no longer your own, you are Christ's.

If you are concerned that you may be a demon-possessed Christian, and want to change, it's not worth holding on to your life as it is. God has so much more for you. If you are humble enough to admit that all you have tried so far to find spiritual freedom has not worked, God is ready to heal you and deliver you right now. It is not a matter of when God wants to set you free; it's a matter of when are you ready to do what it takes to be free?

God's love is immense and unimaginable, and His mercy is far greater than we could ever comprehend. Even if you have made Him small in your eyes for many years, doubting His goodness or His willingness to rescue you from your enemies, He wants to show you just how much He can do right now. That's His character, and His love is unchangeable for all eternity. If you seek out your freedom today, He will undoubtedly grant it to you.

"For this reason I bow my knees before the Father, from whom every family in heaven and on earth derives its name, that He would grant you, according to the riches of His glory, to be strengthened with power through His Spirit in the inner man, so that Christ may dwell in your hearts through faith; and that you, being rooted and grounded in love, may be able to comprehend with all the saints what is the breadth and length and height and depth, and to know the love of Christ which surpasses knowledge, that you may be filled up to all the fullness of God. Now to Him who is able to do far more abundantly beyond all that we ask or think, according to the power that works within us, to Him be the glory in the church and in Christ Jesus to all generations forever and ever. Amen" (Ephesians 3:14-21).

Alan's Testimony

For all the Bible verses, explanations, and opinions I have given, it all would be worthless if it didn't really work. Alan Clayton's story, which appears at the beginning of Chapter 6, is just one example of the powerful effect of strong prayers of deliverance joined together with a real understanding of what true faith is and what authority we have right now in Christ. Alan was a possessed believer that appeared to be a hopeless case. He had been abandoned by and even expelled from churches, not only because he was unable to control his addictions, but because pastors were ill-equipped to set him free from his demons. For Jesus, Alan was never a hopeless case, but unfortunately the Church today has little to offer those who are suffering as Alan once was. I add this postscript to reveal just how urgent the need for true deliverance is today, to do what Jesus came for, "…to preach the gospel to the poor…to proclaim release to the captives, and recovery of sight to the blind, to set free those who are oppressed, to proclaim the favorable year of the Lord" (Luke 4:18-19).

I became a "Christian" at age nineteen. Before this my life was a living nightmare. I seemed to live in a continuous fit of rage, and the only things I cared about were drinking, taking LSD, and acting out depraved sexual fantasies. Like most sexual addicts, I was introduced to pornography at a very early age, between the ages of six and eight. Though my parents were good-hearted and kind, they also had very serious problems in their marriage because of alcohol and violence and found it hard to bring us up in a proper way.

When I was fourteen my parents separated and I was pretty much on my own, living in a trailer in the back yard of my father's house so he could be alone to do whatever he wanted. I could have as much sex, drugs, alcohol, and violence as I wanted, and my appetite for these things was insatiable. I couldn't count the number of girls I had slept with—it was as much a daily thing as eating. I could fly off the handle and become ruthlessly violent at a moment's notice. I smashed a friend's hand with a spiked club, I beat up women, and I was arrested and beaten up by police for punching an eight year old while I was on LSD.

I was very creative and interested in art and music, but only in the most violent and radical punk rock music. I started a band called Dead Fresh New Baby Corpse. I was proud of my artistic talent, and I would write lyrics that would just flow out from my hand as if they came from some mystical source. They were all dark and twisted, and their message was always one of despair. My drawings were the same. I would be amazed at the intricate works of art my hands would create. Strange creatures and images would just emerge as if by themselves. Every single one was a painting of misery, torment, and agony, and I even made some money off of them by others who could relate to my perverse view of life.

With all the bitterness and evil in my heart, I had a desire to know about God, and at nineteen I began attending church, although I considered everyone there to be a total hypocrite. But through the patience and kindness of the pastor there, I found that something in church struck a chord in me. I was able to stop the drinking, swearing, and the LSD, but the lust and the violence were too overwhelming to shake. I immersed myself in Bible studies and prayer and had long counseling sessions with the pastor, who tirelessly answered my questions. Though I tried to hide it, my sexual addiction was always right under the surface.

I called myself a Christian, married a young woman at church, and was considered one of the main members of the church, but still these major problems in my life were not taken care of. When my pastor and most of the congregation chose to move out of state, my life started to deteriorate even faster. I felt abandoned by the only people I felt cared for me. Women from the church found out I was having marital problems and appeared out of nowhere, and I plunged back into my sexual addiction deeper than ever before. My marriage ended in divorce.

For the next several years I lived in misery. I was thrown out of churches because of my promiscuous behavior, got involved with a Satanist girlfriend, and became more and more angry and hungry for violence. As the term "road rage" was used more and more to describe the weird behavior of people in Southern California, I was right in the middle of it helping that demon to get into the news. If someone would cut me off in traffic, I would chase him down and find some way to get revenge, even if it meant damaging my own car. One day I chased a guy for miles on the freeway, followed him until he reached a red light, jumped out of my car, and smashed his windshield in his face with a metal club. He was so terrified that he just took off without reporting me. I especially found pleasure in ramming my car into women drivers; I'd wave and smile as if I was sorry and drive away.

Though I did all of these things, I knew they were wrong, not just toward the people I had hurt, but toward God. I would sink into such condemnation and self-hatred when I realized how evil I was that I would become even more destructive. I would get angry with God. I reasoned that I had given my life to Him but He had not done His part to help me become free from the constant torment of my addictions. "Is this all a game to Him?" I'd ask, "If He wants me to live a holy life, then why does He allow the devil to exist and mess up my life? He knows that Satan is much stronger than I am, so why doesn't He do anything about it? If I just had the chance to put God on trial, I'd convict Him. He wouldn't be able to send me to hell because the entire basis of life on earth is unfair!" The more I thought about these things the madder I got at God. I believed in Him and, strangely enough, felt the conviction that the God of the Bible was the true God, but I was convinced that everything around me was unfair. I was convinced that God was cruel, sadistic and untrustworthy.

I moved to Las Vegas and married a musician, a Satanist who had been involved in vampirism and dressed like Mortitia from *The Addams Family*. She was about to become a sex slave for a man she had met on the Internet and had recently become infatuated with a well-known, convicted serial killer; she was so obsessed with him that she was the first person to get a court order to see him in prison. For some strange reason we both called ourselves Christians, but at the same time we were serious sex addicts. I thought it was God's will that we met. My reasoning was that since I couldn't get over my addiction and she couldn't get over hers, we should just be messed up together.

Not long into the marriage I crossed boundaries of sex and rage where I had never gone before and became sado-masochistic. I was unfaithful to my wife, constantly went to adult book stores, cruised around in my car for hours looking at women, did lewd things in public, fantasized about hurting or mutilating women, and even came close to doing it several times. I had an affair with a transsexual and contemplated a long-term relationship with him, but I was plagued with terrible nightmares and couldn't follow through with it. Finally, my second wife divorced me, convinced that I would eventually kill her and our young daughter.

I moved back to California alone and bounced from one job to another, waking up each morning with incredible depression and dealing every day with huge mood swings—from intensely energetic and excited to totally apathetic and suicidal. It was at this point in my life that I met a beautiful girl named Seansay. I didn't know it at the time, but God was going to use her to bring me to my freedom. She was extremely sick from migraines, anxiety, pain all over her body, and insomnia, and I had my addictions to sex and rage. I don't know how either of us survived our childhoods and early adult years; the only explanation is that the Holy Spirit was protecting us through all of our confusion.

I told Seansay everything about my life because I didn't want her getting into something she knew nothing about. But despite all that, she still loved me. She saw a lot of similarities between us and we stuck it out for two years. I thought, "This girl is either crazy or the nicest person I've ever met." She didn't call herself a Christian, but I did. I'd try to tell her about God and that she needed to make Him first in her life, but what kind of example was I? I was under the impression that maybe she could receive Christ and make it to heaven, but that I was doomed, a hopeless case before God. I hated doing the things I did. After each sin I committed I would want to kill myself, but still I couldn't stop sinning. Any time I really tried to bear down and follow God I would be bombarded with sexual attacks. The harder I tried to follow God the worse my addiction seemed to get.

I wrote a lot of love notes to Seansay, and she would often notice strange things about my writing. I'd write about myself in the third person, as if someone else was speaking through me, and I would refer to hidden things and people that should remain hidden. But she passed it off as my weird attempt to be as eccentric as possible—something I prided myself in. It was amazing that with all the problems we both were suffering we got along so well and came to love each other in a deeper way than we had ever experienced.

My first church had taught me that as soon as a person accepts Christ he is freed from demons. Maybe that person could be oppressed, attacked from the outside, but never possessed. I had accepted the Lord Jesus (so I thought), but my life was as demonic as anyone could get! My life wasn't entirely bad. There were times that God blessed me and times when I could even feel His presence in spite of my addiction, but I always blamed Him for not being willing to set me free. When God answered my prayers, even while I was still deep in sin, I was thankful for the blessings. Yet right away I'd begin to get angry with God again because life was getting too good. I was convinced that He was toying with me; every time something good happened, it would be wiped out by something much worse. For some reason I never blamed the devil for the terrible times but believed that God had thrown them at me as punishment.

In March of 2002, even though I loved Seansay so much, things came to a head and we broke up. I was about to be put in prison and even imagined, in some twisted way, that prison would be a good idea, an experience that I'd actually like. But during our separation we were both utterly miserable. I hated life. I hated waking up in the mornings. Even when I was with Seansay I'd have this sadness because of my addiction. She was too good for me. I told myself, "I'm just going to get AIDS and die." It was the worst time of my life. I had lost Seansay and felt there was really nothing to live for.

I was surprised, then, when she called me up one day to invite me to a church meeting. She had seen a TV program late at night while she was tossing and turning in one of her bouts of insomnia. It was the program *Real Answers* from Living Faith Church. She immediately sat up and thought, "These people are talking about me!" They announced a special meeting, and she decided that we should both go because it sounded like this church would be able to help. My attitude was, "I'll try anything one last time and then I'm going to die."

We went to that healing and deliverance meeting, and what impressed me the most was that there was no fluff or hype at Living Faith. Bishop David came out and started to pray right away—and it was heavy. He said that if we as Christians weren't seeing power and healing in our lives, then God would have to be a liar. Either the promises in the Bible are true or God is a sadistic fiend up in the sky playing games with us. Bishop spoke with authority and did not mince words.

When the service was over, Seansay and I made a beeline to talk to him and told him everything about our lives. When we had finished, Bishop simply told us that we were possessed by evil spirits and needed to have them cast out. My first response was amazement—I had never even considered the possibility. But then it made sense, and I said, "Praise God!" I can't tell you what a relief it was to be given a reason for all the garbage in my life! In the past no one would give me a credible explanation for why my life was the way it was. But from that day on my life began to change for the better, and I haven't dared to turn away from this new power and authority that God has given me.

Over the next nine months, Seansay and I faithfully came to the church and to counseling sessions. I manifested demons during the prayers, had them cast out, and learned amazing things about God and His power for us today. Bit by bit the anger and rage that I had for others and for God left, and I began to feel and experience God in a way I had never imagined was possible. My process of deliverance was more than just coming to church to receive prayers; it was learning how to open up my heart to trust in God. God was ready to set me free from the beginning, but I was blocking Him by my refusal to accept His forgiveness and mercy. Maybe it just sounds philosophical for some people, but for me to believe that God really did love me and forgive me despite the rotten things I had done was an incredible obstacle for my faith. I had never experienced real love and acceptance in my life, and I had been convinced through so much rejection and failure that I could never be worthy enough for God to heal me of all my torment. Only through constantly coming to church to learn about God's character, about fighting our enemies, and about the authority we have in Jesus' name did I finally tear down all those walls I had put up against God.

The first few times that Bishop David prayed for me, I'd feel strange things inside myself. I'd feel a rage well up inside of me and a desire to grab Bishop and slam him against the wall or do something violent against him. Of course, I'd hold it back—I couldn't act that way in church with my pastor! But when Bishop asked me how I was feeling during the prayer, if I felt anything strange, I apologized and told him what was going on. He told me that those urges were from the many demons that were hiding inside of my body and that I shouldn't hold back, that I should allow them to manifest! I couldn't believe he actually wanted me to let go, to do what the urges were compelling me to do. I was scared that I would seriously hurt him, but he assured me that it was not a battle of our flesh, but a spiritual one—the power of God was in control and these demons would have to submit. I couldn't figure out how he would be able to handle it, but I obeyed.

When the demons manifested the first time, they were convinced that they were invincible. I was conscious during the manifestation, but it was as if I were pushed into the background while another person was speaking and acting through me. It was a weird experience—not having control over my own body, hearing my own voice speaking, screaming, cursing, and arguing. As Bishop rebuked the demon, I could feel its hatred for the authority that he had in Jesus. I remember the demon feeling confused that it wasn't as all-powerful as it thought it was, that even though it tried to throw Bishop through the wall, it couldn't even budge him from his place. It was trying to grab at his neck and choke him, but when it knew that it didn't have physical strength to go against the presence of God, it began to argue its weird and twisted logic to try and weaken Bishop's faith and resolve: "You can't cast me out, I've been here for a long time. I'm a strong demon here—nothing like those weak little demons you're used to casting out. You think you're so good and holy, you're not strong enough for me!" With each statement, Bishop would continue rebuking it and telling the demon it had no authority and no power.

Bishop could have cast them all out right away, but he wanted to show Seansay and myself just how the devil works. So he asked the demon many questions and allowed it to reveal itself more, just for all of us to learn. The demon began to say, "Hey, guys, this isn't a demon. Its just me, Alan," and all the while the demon had his eyes closed and was physically wrestling with Bishop. "Seansay, honey, let's go home. Bishop, it's late, you have to go home and take care of your kids. Come on, what are you doing? This is just Alan, there are no demons here!" When Bishop would rebuke the evil spirit, it would change its tune, "What do you mean, 'in Jesus' name?' I'm Jesus!" then it would go on ranting and raving, saying whatever it could to throw Bishop off guard or make him weak. But no matter what the various demons said, Bishop always knew that it wasn't his own holiness or perfection that made him able to cast them out; it was by a simple and stubborn faith in the Lord Jesus.

The first time I really manifested and Bishop cast the demons out, I felt so strange—so empty, so alone. I burst into tears and tried to crawl under the desk in Bishop David's office, feeling as if the only companions that had ever been faithful to me were gone. In some perverse way, I had come to depend on those demons as my only true friends. But thanks to all the prayers and words of faith from Bishop and Evelyn, I knew that I wasn't alone or empty, I could fill myself with the Spirit of God instead. I left that day feeling more free and happy than I had ever felt in my life. But there was more to it than that—I had to learn how to have that simple and stubborn faith myself in order to keep these demons out forever.

Seansay was also manifesting demons during the prayers but in a very different way. The demons in her life loved to laugh in an evil, mocking way, and they appeared to be very calm, passive, and undisturbed by anyone's faith. Like mine, they liked to argue and lie, but they weren't violent. They were the cause of all the misery in her childhood, all the physical pains, insomnia, fears, and nervousness that she felt every day. As weeks went by, I was amazed to see the changes that went on in her. It wasn't long before she was totally healed of fibromyalgia and was sleeping well every single night. Her energy levels rose, and she was able to work straight through the day and still be able to run other errands (a simple trip to the post office used to be the most she could handle for a day). Her faith grew and her determination to see both of us free was a constant inspiration and encouragement to me.

Unfortunately, because we were in the process of learning how to truly believe in God, we kept letting these demons back into our lives through things that we never knew were so harmful: our doubts, our fears, unhealthy friendships, worry, anger—just ordinary patterns of behavior that we thought were normal. We had to clean out all the garbage of our past. I put aside my old music and band, and I gave up my artwork. Seansay brought her boxes of Wicca articles to church for the pastors to destroy, and anything else that we felt had become idols in our lives we gave up no matter how valuable they had been to us before.

There were times that both Seansay and I would drag ourselves to church feeling great oppression, fear, and frustration. But after receiving the strong prayers for deliverance, hearing the Word of God, and being in the company of others with the same faith, we would leave feeling free, blessed, and on top of the world. I'd tell myself never to go back to that old way of thinking, that it was total garbage and not worth giving any importance to at all. I'd ask Seansay, "Why did I think like that? How could I have doubted God so much throughout the week?" We would laugh and go back to our daily lives, then, BAM!—we'd get hit again with all the same old tricks of the devil: "You're not good enough…you're not strong enough…you don't have enough faith…you need to take a break from all this praying...you're wasting your time...stop fighting!" And back down into the pit of misery I'd go, feeling like God was a million miles away. The lustful feelings would intensify, the anger, the demonic dreams, the irritation, and the self-condemnation would return—and all the rotten behavior that comes along with them. But with Seansay's encouragement and the memory of what God had done for me through the prayers at Living Faith, we'd drag ourselves back to church again like a couple of beaten up rag dolls, believing that maybe God would forgive us for doubting Him.

Another time that I manifested was after a service, when everyone except Seansay and I had gone home. Only Bishop and his family were there, and I asked for one more prayer before we went home. I was feeling "off," and I knew that evil spirits were still messing me up inside. I didn't know this, but Bishop was determined to make these demons kneel before Jesus over and over again to humiliate them, and teach them a lesson. As I manifested again, fighting and arguing as usual, a lot of things came out. The demon spoke of how proud it was to have destroyed so many generations of my family. It spoke specifically of tragedies that had happened, and it took credit for them, even demanding a plaque in honor of all the perversion and evil it had done in my family. I could see dark clusters hovering over generation after generation, and I could sense that they went back to the time of the Civil War. This demon spoke in a strong southern accent.

When Bishop commanded the demons to kneel, they refused and gave a big fight, but eventually they kneeled to the authority of Jesus name. When he commanded them to get up and kneel again, they were furious! They would hide and I would come back to consciousness, but Bishop would have none of that—they had to obey and leave just as he commanded. By that time we were both sweating and tired, and I felt so sorry for him. I told him I'd kneel before Jesus by myself if that would help, but he explained that it was the will of the demons that he wanted to break, not mine. So as

I closed my eyes, he called the cowardly demons to manifest again, and they returned as angry and stubborn as before. They hated the idea of kneeling before Jesus and begged Bishop just to cast them out, but he wouldn't.

Half an hour went by, and they still refused to kneel again. As Bishop spoke about the sacrifice of Jesus on the cross destroying all the power of the devil, something happened. I believe I was completely unconscious as the demons pulled me out of Bishop's grasp, and I lunged for the door, with Bishop running after me. It was almost one in the morning, and I sped down the road, turned the corner, and headed straight for the freeway—with the intention of throwing myself into the middle of traffic to be run over. I don't remember what happened, but I know that Bishop, Evelyn, and Seansay were all praying for me. They prayed that God would bind up these demons and not allow them to harm me or anything else. I woke up lying on my back in an empty parking lot next to the freeway, with Bishop smiling down at me and helping me to my feet.

The demons were not yet cast out, but they were totally humiliated and hiding inside of me. He walked me back to the church and began praying again. He told the demons that they had proven their weakness by running away and by hiding; they had already revealed that the name of Jesus was far greater than they were, and he cast them out simply and easily. I couldn't believe how wonderful I felt—so ashamed of my lack of faith, but thrilled to be free once again. I wanted more than anything to stay free and to keep my life right with Jesus. A strong conviction came into my heart that, someday, I wanted to help others the same way that I was being helped. I wanted the same freedom for my whole family.

One of the most amazing things for Seansay and I was that, through all the times we fell in our faith, God was always ready to pick us right back up again and set us free by His power and mercy. Falling into sin used to keep me down for weeks. Even though I wanted to repent, I was convinced that God would have nothing to do with me because of what

I had done, and that condemnation would drive me to more self-loathing, which would drive me to indulging in more destructive and evil behavior. I would just spiral downwards into a pit. But in learning about who God really is—from His Word and from the examples of other real Christians around me—I discovered how amazing God's mercy really is. I discovered that I really could get right back on track and that when He forgives it's over and done.

I remember many times calling Bishop in the middle of the night from the bottom of my pit, angry at God again and confused, but knowing that there had to be a way out. He would basically tell me the same simple message that Jesus teaches, but he had to reword it over and over for me to get it through my head: God is powerful, full of love, and ready to change my life right at that moment. He'd pray and rebuke the demons messing with my mind and I would always feel better. Always. As time went on and Seansay and I tried our best to take everything we were taught from the Bible to heart and practice it, the attacks of the devil didn't necessarily become weaker, but we became stronger.

We began to take on the spirit of a warrior who is ruthless against demons. We learned that fighting the devil is a battle on all fronts. We started coming to church every single day of the week, sometimes driving more than an hour through traffic to get to the service on time, but not missing even one. We prayed together every day. We learned how to show love to the worst people while silently rebuking the demons at work inside of them. We learned that patience and humility are big weapons against the devil, that loving those who are difficult to love doesn't mean just letting them get away with whatever they want but sometimes being tough on them. We learned how to speak by faith—something we had never done before—to determine that each day was blessed and good even before it began, that we were healed and free no matter what our bodies or emotions told us, that we lived by faith and not by feelings. We learned how to take hold of the Bible and make it real for our lives; to look at David and

Goliath and say, "That's me, and I'm going to cut off the head of my problems right now!"; to see Gideon and his ridiculously small army and say, "That's me, and I'm going to wipe out this huge multitude of demons by my faith in the Lord Jesus Christ alone!"

And with each answer to our prayers, with each victory, with each miracle God did in our lives, He became so much more real and beautiful and powerful and personal. He was more than just the God that I professed to believe in (as I had done for so many years), He became my close and intimate friend who really cared about all my thoughts and needs. All the anger, rage, lust, fear, and condemnation that I used to have made sense when I realized that it was not just me but demons working in me; as they were cast out, the problems that they brought were cast out, too. Being set free from demons didn't automatically make me pure and perfect, but it has made me able to fill myself with God and really be born again like the Bible says. I've discovered who my true enemy is, and I have no problem being violent and ruthless with the devil, refusing to listen to him, kicking him out of my thoughts and rebuking his plans for my future. In my estimation, here is no other way to live as a Christian. It's either cold or hot; live for God or die. For all the fights I've been in, this daily fight against my flesh, this world, and all of hell brings me the greatest pleasure of all.

As I write this, ten months have gone by since I first came to Living Faith Evangelical Church. If anyone had told me that I could be happy and free in this amount of time, I would never have believed it. I am a truly different person. I look at others who are living like I did and feel so sorry for them. They mock people who enjoy goodness and sweetness and the beauty of God's world, while they think they're so cool—just as I used to. Now I'm on the other side and all their "coolness" is so pitiful and empty to me. All my desires have changed, my character has changed. My direction in life is to serve God and to be a light for everyone around me so they can know how awesome and great God is. Before, I could only hope to be saved by the skin of my teeth. Now I know that there is so much for me to experience and do for His glory. I am beginning a business that I can stick with and develop like nothing else I've ever done. Seansay and I are engaged to be married this year, and we are determined that no matter what sacrifice we have to make, no matter where God calls us to go, we are going to live for Him in a radical way to save others just as we have been saved.

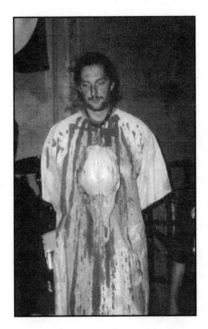

Alan before he was free, dressed up to perform in his band in a blood-stained cloak with a cow's skull around his neck. Obsessed with blood and death, anything but depressing lyrics seemed artificial.

Alan is free from his old addictions, but is still amazed at how God was able to pull him out of such a deep, dark hole.

ENDNOTES

1. *The Nelson Study Bible, NKJV* (Nashville, Tennessee: Thomas Nelson, Inc, 1997), p. 2100.

2. Merriam-Webster's Collegiate Dictionary, 10th edition, p. 310.

3. Vine's Complete Expository Dictionary (Nashville, Tennessee: Thomas Nelson, Inc. 1977), p. 217.

4. J. Lee Grady, "Get Off the Floor," *Charisma & Christian Life* magazine, May 2001, Vol. (Lake Mary Florida, Strang Communications Co.), pp. 8.

Possessed Believers
Order Form

Postal orders: Living Faith Evangelical Church
P.O. Box 3628
Glendale, CA 91221-0628

Telephone orders: (818) 500-7117

Internet orders: www.amazon.com or www.barnesandnoble.com

Please send *Possessed Believers* to:

Name: _____

Address: _____

City: _____ State: _____

Zip: _____

Telephone: (_____) _____

Book Price: $12.00

Shipping: $3.00 for the first book and $1.00 for each additional book to
cover shipping and handling within US, Canada, and Mexico.
International orders add $6.00 for the first book and $2.00 for
each additional book.

Or order from:
ACW Press
85334 Lorane Hwy
Eugene, OR 97405

(800) 931-BOOK

or contact your local bookstore